WHO WANTS TO BE A MILLIONAIRE

THE QUIZ BOOK

WHO WANTS TO BE A MILLIONAIRE

THE QUIZ BOOK

PAN
Pan Macmillan Australia

First published 2000 in Pan by Pan Macmillan Australia Pty Limited
St Martins Tower, 31 Market Street, Sydney

Produced under licence from Celador Productions Limited

National Library of Australia
cataloguing-in-publication data:

Who wants to be a millionaire? The quiz book.

ISBN 0 330 36240 2.

1. Who wants to be a millionaire? (Television programme).
2. Questions and answers. I. Celador International Limited (Firm).
II. Grundy Quizmasters

793.73

Typeset by Post Pre-Press Group
Printed in Australia by Griffin Press

CONTENTS

How to play

Here's the ultimate test all you armchair contestants have been waiting for – nearly a thousand teasers to test every single one of those brain cells. Picture the scene: you've won Fastest Finger First and now you're sitting in the hot-seat under the dimmed lights, ready to start your bid to climb the fifteen levels of the money tree to collect the coveted $1,000,000! You can challenge yourself, or invite some friends around and stage a tournament.

For 1 player

As on *Who Wants To Be A Millionaire?*, the aim of the game is to reach $1,000,000. Start with a question worth $100 and once you have decided on your final answer (and are absolutely sure . . .) follow the page reference at the foot of the page to find out if you've won that amount. If your answer is correct, you can play to win $200 and so on up the tree. The page where the $200 questions (and every other money level) begin is listed in the answer section.

As on the programme you have three lifelines to help you on your way to $1,000,000, these are, of course, optional but each of them can only be used once, so only use them when you really need to.

50:50 Fifty-Fifty

This option takes away two incorrect answers leaving the correct answer and one incorrect answer remaining, a page reference at the bottom of each page will direct you to the relevant section.

Ask The Audience

This works in exactly the same way as on *Who Wants To Be A Millionaire?* except you get to pick your audience! Wherever you are, enlist the help of as many people as you can: if you're at home, switch off the TV for a second, prize your child away from the Playstation and put your family to the test. Or, if you're playing on a bus or train, call on the help of your fellow passengers – they'll probably jump at the chance to relieve the boredom of a long journey. The more people you ask, the higher your chances of choosing the correct answer. Hand around pieces of paper and give your "audience" thirty seconds to write down what they think the answer is. Collect everybody's paper and add up how many people went for each different option. In the end, however, the final decision is yours!

Phone-A-Friend

If you have a telephone handy (and a willing friend!) ring him/her up to help you out. You have thirty seconds (no cheating, now . . .) to read the question to your friend and for them to tell you what they think the answer is. If there's someone else around, ask if they can time it for you.

If you answer incorrectly, you are out of the game. $1,000 and $32,000 are "safe havens" so if you answer a question incorrectly and you have not reached $1,000 then not only are you out of the game but you won't have won a cent! If you have reached one (or both) of these havens and you answer a question incorrectly, then you are out of the game but you will have won the value of the previous haven you have reached. If at any point during the game you are unsure of an answer and don't want to risk losing everything if you answer incorrectly, you can "stick" at the amount you have won so far and that will be your final score. Use the score sheets at the back of the book as you play to keep a running record of the amount you have won and the lifelines you have used.

For 2-5 players

Players should take turns at being "Eddie McGuire" and posing questions to the other contestant/s. The rules are the same as for a single player (see above). The game is over when everyone is out or when someone wins $1,000,000 . . . The first person to reach $1,000,000 wins the game. If no one becomes a millionaire then the player who has won the most money when everyone is out is the winner.

Are you ready to play? Good. With all that money at stake, we're sure we don't need to tell you to think very carefully before you give your final answer. Good luck and be sure to remember at all times the motto of *Who Wants To Be A Millionaire?* – it's only easy if you know the answer!

50:50

15	$1 MILLION
14	$500,000
13	$250,000
12	$125,000
11	$64,000
10	**$32,000**
9	$16,000
8	$8,000
7	$4,000
6	$2,000
5	**$1,000**
4	$500
3	$300
2	$200
1 ◆	**$100**

1 ◆ $100

1

In the Walt Disney film of the same name, what type of creature is Bambi?

- A: Deer
- B: Elephant
- C: Mouse
- D: Cat

2

In which country was the 1992 film 'Strictly Ballroom' set?

- A: South Africa
- B: Canada
- C: New Zealand
- D: Australia

3

In Australia, comradeship as an ideal is known by what name?

- A: Mateship
- B: Buddy system
- C: Equality
- D: Old school tie

4

Who is colloquially known as a 'bookie'?

- A: Bookmaker
- B: Bookkeeper
- C: Bookbinder
- D: Bookseller

5

A huge hit in 1967, what was the name of John Farnham's 'cleaning lady'?

- A: Josie
- B: Sadie
- C: Betty
- D: Milly

If you would like to use your 50:50 please turn to page 239
Turn to the answer section on page 255 to find out if you've won $100!

6

Which of these words is slang for 'money'?

- A: Dosh
- B: Mush
- C: Kudos
- D: Hash

7

A dangerously soft-hearted person is sometimes described as a bleeding what?

- A: Brain
- B: Kidney
- C: Spleen
- D: Heart

8

An Australian invention, the flight memory recorder in an aircraft is better known as the what colour box?

- A: Black
- B: Brown
- C: Yellow
- D: Grey

9

Probably the most famous portrait ever painted is Leonardo da Vinci's 'Mona who'?

- A: Priscilla
- B: Stella
- C: Lisa
- D: Sophia

10

When one is in a hallucinatory state, which animals are said to be pink?

- A: Panthers
- B: Elephants
- C: Aardvarks
- D: Goannas

If you would like to use your 50:50 please turn to page 239
Turn to the answer section on page 255 to find out if you've won $100!

11

Which large structure in New South Wales is colloquially known as the coathanger?

A: Sydney Opera House
B: Sydney Harbour Bridge
C: Anzac Bridge
D: Cahill Expressway

12

From which language do we get the word cappuccino?

A: Italian
B: French
C: German
D: Japanese

13

Which of the following pioneered frozen food production?

A: Clarence Birdseye
B: Henrik Crowsfoot
C: Ivor Nestegg
D: William Duckbill

14

Originally made by Bryant and May of Melbourne, Redheads are a famous brand of which product?

A: Hair dye
B: Ice blocks
C: Matches
D: Toothpicks

15

Which Australian animal has a duck-like bill?

A: Emu
B: Koala
C: Platypus
D: Wombat

If you would like to use your 50:50 please turn to page 239
Turn to the answer section on page 255 to find out if you've won $100!

16

What is the official unit of currency in Japan?

- A: Ben
- B: Hen
- C: Yen
- D: Zen

17

An Australian classic novel by Rolf Boldrewood is 'Robbery Under what'?

- A: Arms
- B: Legs
- C: Water
- D: Pants

18

The habit of denigrating or 'cutting down' those who are successful is often described as the tall what syndrome?

- A: Pansy
- B: Poppy
- C: Polyanthus
- D: Petunia

19

In Australia, scones with jam and cream served with tea or coffee is known as a Devonshire what?

- A: Tea
- B: Treat
- C: Supper
- D: Snack

20

How many legs does a tripod have?

- A: One
- B: Three
- C: Nine
- D: One hundred

If you would like to use your 50:50 please turn to page 239
Turn to the answer section on page 255 to find out if you've won $100!

21

Popular at fetes, a pink and white sweet of icing sugar and desiccated coconut is known as coconut what?

- A: Ice
- B: Roughs
- C: Fudge
- D: Chutney

22

To remain neutral or undecided in a dispute is to sit on the what?

- A: Bench
- B: Fence
- C: Saddle
- D: Gate

23

The abbreviation EFTPOS literally stands for electronic funds transfer at point of what?

- A: Safety
- B: Sale
- C: Station
- D: Stand-off

24

A didgeridoo is made from what material?

- A: Steel
- B: Bone
- C: Wood
- D: Plastic

25

By what name is an elk known in North America?

- A: Heron
- B: Killer whale
- C: Moose
- D: Eel

If you would like to use your 50:50 please turn to page 239
Turn to the answer section on page 255 to find out if you've won $100!

26

Which hat is worn as part of the Australian soldier's uniform?

- A: Sombrero
- B: Deerstalker
- C: Slouch
- D: Boater

27

What is the abbreviation for the organisation, founded in Britain in 1824, to enforce laws to protect animals?

- A: NSPCA
- B: RSPCC
- C: RSPCA
- D: NSPCC

28

The 1984 Australian federal election was contested by Prime Minister Bob Hawke and Opposition leader Andrew who?

- A: Finch
- B: Partridge
- C: Peacock
- D: Wren

29

Mount Gambier's famous Blue Lake turns a brilliant shade of what colour in summer?

- A: Blue
- B: Green
- C: Grey
- D: Yellow

30

Cadbury Schweppes is Australia's leading manufacturer of which product?

- A: Champagne
- B: Cheese
- C: Chocolate
- D: Chop suey

If you would like to use your 50:50 please turn to page 239
Turn to the answer section on page 255 to find out if you've won $100!

31

In an Australian pub, to buy a drink for someone is to what?

A: Roar
B: Scream
C: Shout
D: Yell

32

Which spelling is correct for the word meaning 'a slight hesitation'?

A: PORES
B: PAWS
C: PAUSE
D: POURS

33

Which birds are kept in lofts and used for racing?

A: Chickens
B: Ducks
C: Ostriches
D: Pigeons

34

Which Australian politician was a former television quiz show champion?

A: Barry Jones
B: Jeff Kennett
C: Tim Fischer
D: Pauline Hanson

35

A slab, case or box is a carton of 24 cans of what beverage?

A: Soft drink
B: Beer
C: Fruit juice
D: Milk

If you would like to use your 50:50 please turn to page 239
Turn to the answer section on page 255 to find out if you've won $100!

36

Which of these is not an Australian term for a swimming costume?

A: Togs
B: Bathers
C: Cossie
D: Birthday suit

37

A popular consumer magazine is the 'Australian Women's what'?

A: Daily
B: Weekly
C: Fortnightly
D: Monthly

38

Brothers Tim and Neil Finn led the band Split what?

A: Personalities
B: Peas
C: Hairs
D: Enz

39

Who is the head of the Roman Catholic church?

A: Pope
B: Cardinal
C: Shah
D: Godfather

40

Which title goes before the name of a man who has been knighted?

A: Sir
B: Madam
C: Count
D: Prince

If you would like to use your 50:50 please turn to page 239
Turn to the answer section on page 255 to find out if you've won $100!

41

Who or what would somebody write about in an autobiography?

- A: Themself
- B: A car
- C: Wildlife
- D: The future

42

Which of the following is traditionally associated with a Maypole?

- A: Marriage
- B: Dancing
- C: Barber's shop
- D: Pole-vaulting

43

Which form of transport moves along on a cushion of air?

- A: Monorail
- B: Ferry
- C: Tank
- D: Hovercraft

44

Which part of a book is also a type of finger?

- A: Epilogue
- B: Index
- C: Appendix
- D: Prologue

45

Which of these people might use a rolling pin?

- A: Builder
- B: Fisherman
- C: Gardener
- D: Baker

If you would like to use your 50:50 please turn to page 239
Turn to the answer section on page 255 to find out if you've won $100!

46

Who 'sat in the corner', according to the nursery rhyme?

A: Little Boy Blue
B: Little Jack Horner
C: Little Miss Muffet
D: Little Johnny Green

47

What sort of animal is Walt Disney's 'Dumbo'?

A: Deer
B: Rabbit
C: Elephant
D: Donkey

48

Which group released an album called 'Sergeant Pepper's Lonely Hearts Club Band'?

A: Spice Girls
B: Oasis
C: Rolling Stones
D: Beatles

49

What is the name of Queen Elizabeth II's husband?

A: Prince Michael
B: Prince Planet
C: Prince Charming
D: Prince Philip

50

In which country did spaghetti originate?

A: France
B: Wales
C: Italy
D: Australia

If you would like to use your 50:50 please turn to page 239
Turn to the answer section on page 255 to find out if you've won $100!

51

An admiral is a high-ranking officer in which force?

A: Navy
B: Army
C: Police
D: Air force

52

What is a twelfth of a foot called?

A: A toe
B: An inch
C: A metre
D: A pound

53

Where on the body should a helmet be worn?

A: On the feet
B: Around the waist
C: Between the knees
D: On the head

54

How many seasons are there in a year?

A: Four
B: Six
C: Twelve
D: Twenty four

55

What colour ball should normally be struck by the cue in snooker?

A: Black
B: Mauve
C: Orange
D: White

If you would like to use your 50:50 please turn to page 239
Turn to the answer section on page 255 to find out if you've won $100!

56

Which part of a lettuce is usually eaten in salads?

- A: Seeds
- B: Roots
- C: Berries
- D: Leaves

57

What is another name for a moving staircase?

- A: Elevator
- B: Escalator
- C: Perambulator
- D: Rotavator

58

How would a musician play a triangle?

- A: Suck it
- B: Blow it
- C: Pluck it
- D: Strike it

59

Which of these does a horse rider sit on?

- A: Stirrup
- B: Spur
- C: Saddle
- D: Throne

60

Which fictional little girl explored Wonderland?

- A: Alice
- B: Madeline
- C: Violet Elizabeth Bott
- D: Matilda

If you would like to use your 50:50 please turn to page 239
Turn to the answer section on page 255 to find out if you've won $100!

1 ◆ $100

61

The ostrich is the largest example of which group of creatures?

A: Birds
B: Frogs
C: Reptiles
D: Insects

62

What do we call the act of thumbing a lift?

A: Hitch-hiking
B: Camping
C: Joyriding
D: Orienteering

63

Which of these is not the colour of a snooker ball?

A: Blue
B: Yellow
C: Red
D: Purple

64

What is the main item stored in a camel's hump?

A: Sand
B: Pyjamas
C: Maps
D: Fat

65

Which of these animals does not belong to the cat family?

A: Cheetah
B: Leopard
C: Rottweiler
D: Tiger

If you would like to use your 50:50 please turn to page 239
Turn to the answer section on page 255 to find out if you've won $100!

66

Which of these is a prickly plant that usually grows in the desert?

A: Cactus
B: Daffodil
C: Hyacinth
D: Begonia

67

What would you do with a truffle?

A: Play it
B: Wear it
C: Spend it
D: Eat it

68

In Aussie rhyming slang, what are your mince pies?

A: Ears
B: Eyes
C: Mouth
D: Nose

69

The Jason Reclina is synonymous in Australia with which furniture item?

A: Banana lounge
B: Lounge chair
C: Dining table
D: Water bed

70

A northern Australian marine crustacean popular as food is the Moreton Bay what?

A: Beetle
B: Bug
C: Creepy
D: Crawly

If you would like to use your 50:50 please turn to page 239
Turn to the answer section on page 255 to find out if you've won $100!

71

What is an Australian colloquial contraction of afternoon?

A: Arfto
B: Arvo
C: Ternoon
D: PM

72

A classic Australian song is 'Click Go the what'?

A: Scissors
B: Secateurs
C: Shears
D: Castanets

73

What was the name of the baby who disappeared from an Uluru camping ground in August 1980?

A: Antonia
B: Azaria
C: Amelia
D: Alison

74

Until 1984, what was Australia's official national anthem?

A: Rule Britannia
B: Waltzing Matilda
C: Land of Hope and Glory
D: God Save the Queen

75

Proclaimed in 1984, the official colours of Australia are green and which other?

A: Gold
B: White
C: Red
D: Blue

If you would like to use your 50:50 please turn to page 239
Turn to the answer section on page 255 to find out if you've won $100!

76

Anything wonderful or first rate is often described as the greatest thing since sliced what?

- A: Salami
- B: Bread
- C: Cheese
- D: Corned beef

77

In which industry is Hoyts a famous Australian name?

- A: Cinema
- B: Ice cream
- C: Fast food
- D: Light rail

78

Promoting Australian tourism, Paul Hogan would say 'throw another what on the barbie'?

- A: Shrimp
- B: Chop
- C: Steak
- D: Sausage

79

The abbreviation J.P. literally stands for Justice of the what?

- A: Parole
- B: Police
- C: Peace
- D: Parliament

80

Artist Kevin Hart is best known by what nickname?

- A: Pro
- B: Doc
- C: Turps
- D: Leonardo

If you would like to use your 50:50 please turn to page 239
Turn to the answer section on page 255 to find out if you've won $100!

81

Remembrance Day is observed on which date in November?

A: 1st
B: 11th
C: 15th
D: 29th

82

A drinking tour at a series of hotels in the one outing is called a pub what?

A: Attack
B: Binge
C: Crawl
D: Cruise

83

In Australia, what is a lottery in which the prize is a chicken?

A: Chook raffle
B: Fowl contest
C: Chicken prix
D: Hen's night

84

According to a classic Australian song, 'Kookaburra sits on the old what'?

A: Man's head
B: Gum tree
C: Picket fence
D: Shed out the back

85

Australian Wally Lewis was a champion in which sport?

A: Australian Rules
B: Boxing
C: Rugby League
D: Netball

If you would like to use your 50:50 please turn to page 239
Turn to the answer section on page 255 to find out if you've won $100!

86

James Reyne was lead singer for the rock band Australian what?

- A: Salute
- B: Crawl
- C: Rules
- D: Drawl

87

What is Australian tennis champion John Newcombe's nickname?

- A: Scud
- B: Johnno
- C: Fitzy
- D: Newk

88

Actor Lorraine Bayly played the beloved character Grace, in which popular Australian TV series?

- A: All Together Now
- B: The Bob Morrison Show
- C: Hey Dad!
- D: The Sullivans

89

In what direction is the Gold Coast from Brisbane?

- A: East
- B: North
- C: South
- D: West

90

An Australian exclamation of astonishment is 'stone the what'?

- A: Emus
- B: Galahs
- C: Crows
- D: Cockatoos

If you would like to use your 50:50 please turn to page 239
Turn to the answer section on page 255 to find out if you've won $100!

91

An Australian silent film of 1916 is 'Mutiny on the what'?

A: Beagle
B: Bounty
C: Endeavour
D: Murray

92

The remote and inland country of Australia is known as the what?

A: Background
B: Backyard
C: Hinterback
D: Outback

93

Which of these sportsmen is a champion of Australian Rugby League?

A: Polly Farmer
B: Ron Barassi
C: Clive Churchill
D: Charlie Yankos

94

Who is the widow of Australian tycoon Robert Holmes à Court?

A: Janet
B: Megan
C: Susan
D: Tracy

95

What particular Australian term describes a trouble-maker?

A: Lackey
B: Larrikin
C: Layabout
D: Lorikeet

If you would like to use your 50:50 please turn to page 239
Turn to the answer section on page 255 to find out if you've won $100!

96

Fremantle is a city within the metropolitan area of which Australian state capital?

A: Adelaide
B: Brisbane
C: Hobart
D: Perth

97

In 1972, Australia's Helen Reddy had a huge hit with the song 'I am what'?

A: Strong
B: Invincible
C: Woman
D: What I Am

98

The 'baggy green cap' is associated with the Australian national team of which sport?

A: Rugby League
B: Cricket
C: Rugby Union
D: Soccer

99

An Australian expression for moving very quickly is to be like a what up a drain pipe?

A: Rat
B: Mole
C: Hamster
D: Gerbil

100

A famous ice-skating partnership is Torvill and who?

A: Bishop
B: Vicar
C: Dean
D: Parson

If you would like to use your 50:50 please turn to page 239
Turn to the answer section on page 255 to find out if you've won $100!

1 ◆ $100

101

What mode of transport is traditionally used by witches in fairy tales?

A: Penny-farthing
B: Scooter
C: Broomstick
D: Unicycle

102

What does a display of 'five o'clock shadow' warrant?

A: Shave
B: Haircut
C: Sunbathe
D: Scrub down

103

According to the proverb, 'Every dog has what'?

A: Bad breath
B: Fleas
C: His day
D: A cold wet nose

104

What kind of eagle is the national bird of the USA?

A: One-legged
B: Hairy
C: Bald
D: Red-nosed

105

What is the name of the famous bell in the clock tower at the Houses of Parliament in London?

A: Big Time
B: Big Bang
C: Big Ben
D: Big Noise

If you would like to use your 50:50 please turn to page 239
Turn to the answer section on page 255 to find out if you've won $100!

106

Which of these boys' names is also a herb?

A: Bertram
B: Basil
C: Boris
D: Bartholomew

107

Which English soccer club shares its name with Bill Clinton's daughter?

A: Arsenal
B: Chelsea
C: Newcastle
D: Watford

108

Which of these was a leader of the Sioux at the Battle of the Little Bighorn?

A: Sitting Up
B: Sitting Bull
C: Sitting Duck
D: Sitting Pretty

109

What is a hundredth of a metre called?

A: Centimetre
B: Gram
C: Litre
D: Inch

110

Who married Fred Flintstone?

A: Wilma
B: Barney
C: Pebbles
D: Dino

If you would like to use your 50:50 please turn to page 239
Turn to the answer section on page 255 to find out if you've won $100!

15		$1 MILLION
14		$500,000
13		$250,000
12		$125,000
11		$64,000
10		$32,000
9		$16,000
8		$8,000
7		$4,000
6		$2,000
5		$1,000
4		$500
3		$300
2	◆	$200
1	◆	$100

2 ◆ $200

1

According to folklore, what does the sandman help children to do?

A: Sleep
B: Grow
C: Cross the road
D: Build sandcastles

2

On TV since 1959, puppeteer Norman Hetherington's most famous creation is Mr who?

A: Squiggle
B: Doodle
C: Dotty
D: Graffiti

3

In which sport do Australian and New Zealand teams contest the Bledisloe Cup?

A: Rugby Union
B: Soccer
C: Hockey
D: Rugby League

4

By what name is a cantaloupe more commonly known in Australia?

A: Mandarin
B: Rockmelon
C: Pawpaw
D: Watermelon

5

Dramatically declining in numbers since the mid-1980s, one of the main species of fish caught off Australia's south-east coast is the orange what?

A: Smoothy
B: Shiny
C: Scaly
D: Roughy

If you would like to use your 50:50 please turn to page 240
Turn to the answer section on page 255 to find out if you've won $200!

6

As what is saccharin mainly used?

A: Adhesive
B: Sweetener
C: Whitener
D: Solvent

7

Who starred in the films 'Saturday Night Fever' and 'Pulp Fiction'?

A: John Travolta
B: Samuel L. Jackson
C: Bruce Willis
D: Tim Roth

8

Founded in Newcastle in 1930, a social welfare organisation and religious order of the Anglican Church is the Brotherhood of Saint who?

A: Gregory
B: Stephen
C: Laurence
D: Thomas

9

A prominent Melbourne newspaper is 'The what'?

A: Age
B: Gauge
C: Page
D: Sage

10

Which sign of the zodiac has a sting in the tail?

A: Sagittarius
B: Aries
C: Cancer
D: Scorpio

If you would like to use your 50:50 please turn to page 240
Turn to the answer section on page 255 to find out if you've won $200!

11

An outrageous Australian stand-up comedian is Rodney who?

A: Naughty
B: Bawdy
C: Ribald
D: Rude

12

Which word can mean to gulp down food, to fasten or to break away?

A: Bang
B: Buck
C: Blow
D: Bolt

13

What is the first name of the horticulturist host of TV's 'Burke's Backyard'?

A: Ron
B: Jon
C: Don
D: Con

14

Andrew Gaze is an Australian champion in which sport?

A: Australian Rules
B: Basketball
C: Cricket
D: Rugby League

15

Joh Bjelke-Petersen was a premier of which Australian state?

A: New South Wales
B: Queensland
C: Tasmania
D: Western Australia

If you would like to use your 50:50 please turn to page 240
Turn to the answer section on page 255 to find out if you've won $200!

16

Which of these mountains is the highest?

A: Everest
B: Ben Nevis
C: Mont Blanc
D: Snowdon

17

In tennis, what name is given to a service so good that the opponent fails to touch it?

A: Deuce
B: Advantage
C: Ace
D: Let

18

Which of these is an American TV police drama?

A: NYPD Black
B: NYPD White
C: NYPD Green
D: NYPD Blue

19

What sort of person could be described as an extrovert?

A: Shy
B: Clumsy
C: Greedy
D: Socially confident

20

In Australian vernacular, to wander around the country in a nomadic manner is to go what?

A: AWOL
B: Wandering
C: Walkabout
D: Dutch

If you would like to use your 50:50 please turn to page 240
Turn to the answer section on page 255 to find out if you've won $200!

2 ◆ $200

21

Whose 'Thriller' album is one of the biggest selling records of all time?

A: Michael Jackson
B: Madonna
C: Dire Straits
D: Elvis Presley

22

The Australian tennis men's doubles specialists Mark Woodforde and Todd Woodbridge are collectively known as 'The what'?

A: Woods
B: Woodies
C: Woodsters
D: Woodmeisters

23

What can be 'right', 'acute' or 'reflex'?

A: Accent
B: Lens
C: Angle
D: Edge

24

Which English town is famous for its salts and its racecourse?

A: Epsom
B: Ascot
C: Fontwell
D: Sandown

25

Who played the title role in the film 'Taxi Driver'?

A: Robert De Niro
B: Harvey Keitel
C: Al Pacino
D: James Caan

If you would like to use your 50:50 please turn to page 240
Turn to the answer section on page 255 to find out if you've won $200!

26

Which apparatus is used for weaving?

A: Spinning wheel
B: Sewing machine
C: Loom
D: Knitting needles

27

What is one doing when 'chucking a wobbly'?

A: Bowling a cricket ball
B: Throwing a tantrum
C: Stumbling drunkenly
D: Throwing up

28

Which word means an accidental success?

A: Fluke
B: Fluff
C: Flop
D: Flute

29

What is the opposite of 'temporary'?

A: Residential
B: Permanent
C: Infinite
D: Makeshift

30

To what did the singer Charles Berry change his first name?

A: Chuck
B: Dave
C: Cliff
D: Hank

If you would like to use your 50:50 please turn to page 240
Turn to the answer section on page 255 to find out if you've won $200!

31

Which of these TV-based movies starred Tom Cruise?

- A: Lost In Space
- B: The Saint
- C: Mission Impossible
- D: The Fugitive

32

What name is given to wool immediately after it is removed from a sheep?

- A: Pelt
- B: Hide
- C: Fleece
- D: Down

33

According to the famous proverb, where should you not 'look a gift horse'?

- A: In the eyes
- B: In the mouth
- C: On the hoof
- D: Between the ears

34

Which allergy to pollen affects many people during the summer?

- A: Shingles
- B: Hay fever
- C: Prickly heat
- D: Migraine

35

What sort of travel is associated with Cape Canaveral?

- A: Space
- B: Sea
- C: Rail
- D: Road

If you would like to use your 50:50 please turn to page 240
Turn to the answer section on page 255 to find out if you've won $200!

36

'AD' after a date signifies the number of years after the birth of whom?

- A: Adam
- B: God
- C: Moses
- D: Jesus Christ

37

Which of the following is a large stone circle on Salisbury Plain in England?

- A: Hadrian's Wall
- B: Stonehenge
- C: The 12 Apostles
- D: Ayers Rock

38

Which country was the setting for the TV series 'The Waltons'?

- A: USA
- B: Scotland
- C: New Zealand
- D: Australia

39

What type of flag is shown to the winner of a Grand Prix motor race?

- A: Yellow
- B: Union Jack
- C: Chequered
- D: Striped

40

Which type of instrument is a trombone?

- A: Brass
- B: Woodwind
- C: String
- D: Percussion

If you would like to use your 50:50 please turn to page 240
Turn to the answer section on page 255 to find out if you've won $200!

41

Where on the body is the nape?

A: Leg
B: Chest
C: Arm
D: Neck

42

Which word can follow 'conger' and 'electric'?

A: Shark
B: Snake
C: Eel
D: Lamprey

43

What is a hydrofoil?

A: Sea vessel
B: Aeroplane
C: Racing car
D: Space rocket

44

Where would you wear galoshes?

A: On the head
B: On the hands
C: On the feet
D: Around the waist

45

Which bloodsucking creatures were once commonly used by doctors?

A: Vampire bats
B: Leeches
C: Mosquitoes
D: Snakes

If you would like to use your 50:50 please turn to page 240
Turn to the answer section on page 255 to find out if you've won $200!

46

What sort of food is a bagel?

A: Fruit
B: Bread roll
C: Sausage
D: Fish

47

Which surname connects movie stars Henry, Peter, Jane and Bridget?

A: Barrymore
B: Fonda
C: Russell
D: Ford

48

What does 'surly' mean?

A: Certainly
B: Over
C: Bad-tempered
D: Dirty

49

Which word means a signed document in support of a particular action?

A: Partition
B: Position
C: Perforation
D: Petition

50

What name is given to scribblings or drawings on public walls?

A: Plasterwork
B: Graphicacy
C: Pointing
D: Graffiti

If you would like to use your 50:50 please turn to page 240
Turn to the answer section on page 255 to find out if you've won $200!

51

The Sydney suburb of Randwick has long been associated with which sport?

A: Horse racing
B: Tennis
C: Cricket
D: Surfing

52

What name applies to both a flower and the widow of West Australian mining magnate Lang Hancock?

A: Daisy
B: Hyacinth
C: Rose
D: Violet

53

Which ubiquitous machine was originally known as a fruit machine?

A: Automatic teller
B: Drink
C: Train ticket
D: Poker

54

Sydney's Taronga Park is what kind of institution?

A: Museum
B: Planetarium
C: Zoo
D: Amusement park

55

The phrase 'great Australian dream' refers to the desire to own one's own what?

A: Home
B: Car
C: Boat
D: Television

If you would like to use your 50:50 please turn to page 240
Turn to the answer section on page 255 to find out if you've won $200!

56

Beginning in Warrnambool, Victoria, a famous name in clothing manufacture is Fletcher who?

A: Smith
B: Brown
C: White
D: Jones

57

What is Rolf Harris's trademark musical instrument?

A: Gum leaf
B: Wobble board
C: Comb
D: Lagerphone

58

The acronym HECS stands for Higher Education what Scheme?

A: Co-operative
B: Contribution
C: Contract
D: Compulsory

59

Which part of the body is used as a command for a dog to walk close by its owner?

A: Foot
B: Toe
C: Heel
D: Ankle

60

A large and aggressive Australian ant is the what ant?

A: Angry
B: Bull
C: Cow
D: Belliger

If you would like to use your 50:50 please turn to page 240
Turn to the answer section on page 255 to find out if you've won $200!

61

A 1983 Australian film starring Wendy Hughes is 'Careful, He Might what'?

A: Hear You
B: Hurt You
C: Kill You
D: See You

62

In which Australian state or territory are the Blue Mountains?

A: New South Wales
B: Northern Territory
C: South Australia
D: Western Australia

63

A famous Australian stage singer is Marina who?

A: Anthony
B: Byrne
C: Prior
D: Warlow

64

Who was the partner of Australian rock star Michael Hutchence at the time of his death?

A: Helena Christensen
B: Kylie Minogue
C: Kym Wilson
D: Paula Yates

65

Havana is the capital of which country?

A: Haiti
B: Cuba
C: Mexico
D: Puerto Rico

If you would like to use your 50:50 please turn to page 240
Turn to the answer section on page 255 to find out if you've won $200!

66

Papoose is a North American Indian term for which of these?

- A: Tent
- B: Baby
- C: Slippers
- D: Headdress

67

What is the eighth month of the year?

- A: August
- B: September
- C: October
- D: November

68

What is a piña colada?

- A: Tree
- B: Parrot
- C: Nut
- D: Drink

69

How many years are there in three-quarters of a century?

- A: 50
- B: 65
- C: 75
- D: 80

70

In Roman numerals, which letter represents the number five?

- A: V
- B: X
- C: M
- D: L

If you would like to use your 50:50 please turn to page 240
Turn to the answer section on page 255 to find out if you've won $200!

71

Alitalia is the national airline of which country?

- A: Italy
- B: Sweden
- C: Portugal
- D: France

72

The word 'canine' refers to which animal?

- A: Cat
- B: Rat
- C: Hog
- D: Dog

73

With which sport do you associate Ian Botham?

- A: Rugby League
- B: Tennis
- C: Cricket
- D: Golf

74

Which colour do you associate with being sad and melancholy?

- A: Blue
- B: Purple
- C: Green
- D: Yellow

75

Which Beatle married Yoko Ono in 1969?

- A: George Harrison
- B: Ringo Starr
- C: Paul McCartney
- D: John Lennon

If you would like to use your 50:50 please turn to page 240
Turn to the answer section on page 255 to find out if you've won $200!

76

What is the capital of Spain?

A: Monrovia
B: Munich
C: Madrid
D: Melbourne

77

Which South American country shares its name with a nut?

A: Chile
B: Brazil
C: Ecuador
D: Peru

78

Which branch of medicine is concerned with the treatment of children?

A: Radiology
B: Geriatrics
C: Paediatrics
D: Cardiology

79

Which surname connects film actresses Bette, Geena and Judy?

A: Davis
B: Ford
C: Huston
D: Russell

80

Who would traditionally sing a shanty?

A: Tinker
B: Tailor
C: Soldier
D: Sailor

If you would like to use your 50:50 please turn to page 240
Turn to the answer section on page 255 to find out if you've won $200!

81

The word 'cardiac' means of or relating to which organ of the body?

A: Brain
B: Lung
C: Heart
D: Skin

82

What was the first name of the Spanish artist Dali?

A: Jose
B: Pedro
C: Iago
D: Salvador

83

Cuba is about one hundred miles away from which US state?

A: Alaska
B: California
C: Florida
D: Montana

84

Who was the frequent film partner of Ginger Rogers?

A: Spencer Tracy
B: Mickey Rooney
C: Fred Astaire
D: Stan Laurel

85

Which planet shares its name with a metallic element?

A: Pluto
B: Mercury
C: Jupiter
D: Saturn

If you would like to use your 50:50 please turn to page 240
Turn to the answer section on page 255 to find out if you've won $200!

86

What is the relation of your father's brother's child to you?

A: Uncle
B: Half-brother
C: Second cousin
D: First cousin

87

Which of these is not a type of hat?

A: Bowler
B: Batter
C: Boater
D: Beret

88

Which literary character has a pet called a pushmi-pullyu?

A: Dr Who
B: Dr Finlay
C: Dr Dolittle
D: Dr Jekyll

89

What is helium?

A: Metal
B: Gas
C: Plant
D: Gemstone

90

A Quentin Tarantino film is 'Reservoir what'?

A: Frogs
B: Horses
C: Moles
D: Dogs

If you would like to use your 50:50 please turn to page 240
Turn to the answer section on page 255 to find out if you've won $200!

91

What sort of pastries do you associate with the Queen of Hearts?

- A: Vanilla Slice
- B: Croissants
- C: Pies
- D: Tarts

92

Which trophy is contested by the winners of the AFC and NFC in American Football?

- A: Super Cup
- B: Super Dish
- C: Super Bowl
- D: Super Plate

93

Which spirit lived in Aladdin's lamp?

- A: Genie
- B: Pixie
- C: Goblin
- D: Troll

94

Which season of the year is associated with hibernation?

- A: Spring
- B: Summer
- C: Autumn
- D: Winter

95

Which of these was not one of the famous Marx Brothers?

- A: Groucho
- B: Karl
- C: Chico
- D: Harpo

If you would like to use your 50:50 please turn to page 240
Turn to the answer section on page 255 to find out if you've won $200!

96

With which type of music was Tammy Wynette associated?

A: Opera
B: Country
C: Jazz
D: Folk

97

For what would a wok normally be used?

A: Sailing
B: Fishing
C: Cooking
D: Sleeping

98

What is the specific name for a person who hides aboard a ship or aircraft to get free passage?

A: Stowaway
B: Castaway
C: Runaway
D: Faraway

If you would like to use your 50:50 please turn to page 240
Turn to the answer section on page 255 to find out if you've won $200!

50:50

15		$1 MILLION
14		$500,000
13		$250,000
12		$125,000
11		$64,000
10		$32,000
9		$16,000
8		$8,000
7		$4,000
6		$2,000
5		$1,000
4		$500
3	◆	$300
2	◆	$200
1	◆	$100

3 ◆ $300

1

What do you do if you 'grease someone's palm'?

- A: Tell a fortune
- B: Bribe someone
- C: Give a warning
- D: Shake hands

2

What is used to hit the ball in a game of croquet?

- A: Racquet
- B: Bat
- C: Foot
- D: Mallet

3

Babe Ruth was famous for playing which sport?

- A: Ice Hockey
- B: American Football
- C: Basketball
- D: Baseball

4

Which professionals are called 'realtors' in the USA?

- A: Undertakers
- B: Lawyers
- C: Estate agents
- D: Bankers

5

In which classic TV western series did Lorne Greene play Ben Cartwright?

- A: Bonanza
- B: The High Chaparral
- C: The Virginian
- D: Alias Smith and Jones

If you would like to use your 50:50 please turn to page 242
Turn to the answer section on page 256 to find out if you've won $300!

6

Who played Thelma in the film 'Thelma and Louise'?

- A: Geena Davis
- B: Annette Bening
- C: Juliette Lewis
- D: Sally Field

7

What is a yak?

- A: Sweet potato
- B: Muslim veil
- C: Boat
- D: Long-haired Tibetan ox

8

Featured as a Mad Max movie theme is Tina Turner's 'We Don't Need Another what'?

- A: Madman
- B: Price rise
- C: Politician
- D: Hero

9

To which group of people was Senator Don Chipp referring when he said the Democrats were there 'to keep the bastards honest'?

- A: Major political parties
- B: Police
- C: Trade unions
- D: Big business

10

Who invented psychoanalysis?

- A: Lucien Freud
- B: Clement Freud
- C: Emma Freud
- D: Sigmund Freud

If you would like to use your 50:50 please turn to page 242
Turn to the answer section on page 256 to find out if you've won $300!

3 ◆ $300

11

In traditional Aboriginal ritual practice, to point the bone at another is to intend what result?

- A: Good fortune
- B: Fertility
- C: Recovery from illness
- D: Death

12

In pre-decimal currency, a shilling was known by what boy's name?

- A: Tom
- B: Dick
- C: Harry
- D: Bob

13

In the USA, what are Yellowstone and Yosemite?

- A: Great Lakes
- B: Ivy League Colleges
- C: New York Boroughs
- D: National Parks

14

A short, light surfboard usually ridden lying down, is a what board?

- A: Boogie
- B: Disco
- C: Woogie
- D: Boofy

15

At what distance is Australian swimmer Kieren Perkins an Olympic gold medallist?

- A: 100 metres
- B: 200 metres
- C: 400 metres
- D: 1500 metres

If you would like to use your 50:50 please turn to page 242
Turn to the answer section on page 256 to find out if you've won $300!

3 ◆ $300

16

Which first name goes before Bull, Dory and O'Groats?

A: Jim
B: Jack
C: John
D: Jane

17

As what was Liberace famous?

A: Bullfighter
B: Pianist
C: Footballer
D: Soldier

18

The years from 1929 to the mid-'30s are known for the Great what?

A: Depression
B: Slowdown
C: Recession
D: Bust

19

Glucose is a form of which substance?

A: Salt
B: Sugar
C: Acid
D: Oil

20

On which special day do many people attend a Dawn Service?

A: Melbourne Cup
B: Eight-hour
C: Australia
D: Anzac

If you would like to use your 50:50 please turn to page 242
Turn to the answer section on page 256 to find out if you've won $300!

21

The acronym RAAF stands for Royal Australian what?

A: Air Force
B: Armed Fighters
C: Arts Foundation
D: Association Football

22

What nickname is traditionally given to the clubhouse bar on a golf course?

A: 10th hole
B: 14th hole
C: 18th hole
D: 19th hole

23

Which holiday marks the traditional opening of Australia's ski season?

A: Australia Day
B: Good Friday
C: Queen's Birthday
D: Christmas Day

24

What name is given to the path of one body in space around another?

A: Ambit
B: Orbit
C: Gambit
D: Audit

25

Pyrotechnics means a display of what?

A: Aircraft
B: Fireworks
C: Acrobats
D: Animals

If you would like to use your 50:50 please turn to page 242
Turn to the answer section on page 256 to find out if you've won $300!

26

Which Australian film critic is known as 'Mr Movies'?

- A: Lawrie Zion
- B: David Stratton
- C: Bill Collins
- D: Margaret Pomeranz

27

Which tool is used for spreading mortar?

- A: Mattock
- B: Hoe
- C: Trowel
- D: Spade

28

Made in Australia, the arrowroot is a type of which product?

- A: Arrow
- B: Biscuit
- C: Soft Drink
- D: Beer

29

The sequel to the Australian hit film 'Babe' is 'Babe: Pig in the what'?

- A: City
- B: Middle
- C: Pen
- D: Poke

30

What does 'ambience' mean?

- A: Unhappiness
- B: Atmosphere
- C: Indifference
- D: Nutrition

If you would like to use your 50:50 please turn to page 242
Turn to the answer section on page 256 to find out if you've won $300!

31

In Australia, Onkaparinga is synonymous with which product?

A: Lilo
B: Blanket
C: Mattress
D: Sleeping bag

32

Australia's tallest building, Centrepoint Tower, is in which city?

A: Canberra
B: Melbourne
C: Sydney
D: Hobart

33

Which shoes were first worn by North American Indians?

A: Clogs
B: Sabots
C: Sandals
D: Moccasins

34

In which sport did Mark Spitz win a record seven gold medals at the 1972 Olympics?

A: Skiing
B: Weightlifting
C: Gymnastics
D: Swimming

35

Historically, which of these was particularly associated with the cavalry?

A: Parachutes
B: Tanks
C: Cannons
D: Horses

If you would like to use your 50:50 please turn to page 242
Turn to the answer section on page 256 to find out if you've won $300!

36

Which word commonly goes before 'foot', 'back' and 'faced' to make three new words?

A: Black
B: Big
C: Bare
D: Broad

37

What is Sarah, Duchess of York's maiden name?

A: Phillips
B: Cavendish
C: Rhys-Jones
D: Ferguson

38

Which of these television series featured Kermit the Frog?

A: Here's Humphrey
B: The Munsters
C: The Muppet Show
D: Melrose Place

39

Which word commonly goes before 'delight' and 'bath'?

A: Dutch
B: Greek
C: Turkish
D: Romanian

40

Which famous mountain overlooks Rio de Janeiro?

A: Sugar Loaf
B: Currant Bun
C: Sponge Finger
D: Fairy Cake

If you would like to use your 50:50 please turn to page 242
Turn to the answer section on page 256 to find out if you've won $300!

41

Which flowers were the subject of several famous paintings by Vincent van Gogh?

A: Venus flytraps
B: Sunflowers
C: Snapdragons
D: Daffodils

42

Which stone is also the name of a small round ball of glass?

A: Basalt
B: Granite
C: Limestone
D: Marble

43

Who is Ryan O'Neal's Oscar-winning daughter?

A: Shirley
B: Tatum
C: Bridget
D: Carrie

44

How many lines are there in a limerick?

A: 2
B: 4
C: 5
D: 8

45

What is the collective term for the group of directors who run a large company?

A: Council
B: Cabinet
C: Board
D: Panel

If you would like to use your 50:50 please turn to page 242
Turn to the answer section on page 256 to find out if you've won $300!

46

In the USA, what was outlawed by 'Prohibition'?

- A: Gambling
- B: Drinking alcohol
- C: Smoking
- D: Slavery

47

Somebody described as 'butterfingers' would have a propensity for what?

- A: Being clumsy
- B: Gardening
- C: Playing the piano
- D: Cookery

48

How many hours from Tulsa was Gene Pitney in his 1963 hit song?

- A: 12
- B: 24
- C: 36
- D: 48

49

The substance used to make casts is known as 'Plaster of . . . ' what?

- A: Parramatta
- B: Prague
- C: Perth
- D: Paris

50

In area, what is Australia's largest state?

- A: New South Wales
- B: Queensland
- C: South Australia
- D: Western Australia

If you would like to use your 50:50 please turn to page 242
Turn to the answer section on page 256 to find out if you've won $300!

51

In what Australian state is the famous horse race, the Caulfield Cup run?

A: New South Wales
B: Victoria
C: Queensland
D: Tasmania

52

An Australian Olympic gold medal cyclist is Kathy who?

A: Amp
B: Ohm
C: Volt
D: Watt

53

Glenn Shorrock was lead singer for the what River Band?

A: Big
B: Deep
C: Little
D: Shallow

54

A famous Sydney horse race for 2-year-olds is the Golden what?

A: Slipper
B: Pump
C: Stiletto
D: Boot

55

In what month of the year 2000 was the GST introduced in Australia?

A: January
B: June
C: July
D: December

If you would like to use your 50:50 please turn to page 242
Turn to the answer section on page 256 to find out if you've won $300!

56

At the 1994 Commonwealth Games, Cathy Freeman's victory celebration on the track involved carrying the Australian flag and which other flag?

A: Aboriginal
B: Eureka
C: Chequered
D: Olympic

57

'Diaper' is the North American term for what?

A: Scarf
B: Nappy
C: Tap
D: Jumper

58

Which of these animals is also Aussie rhyming slang for a piano?

A: Goanna
B: Kangaroo
C: Taipan
D: Dingo

59

Its vineyards located in Victoria, an Australian sparkling wine is Great what?

A: Eastern
B: Northern
C: Southern
D: Western

60

A controversial South Australian copper and uranium mine is Roxby what?

A: River
B: Meadows
C: Hill
D: Downs

If you would like to use your 50:50 please turn to page 242
Turn to the answer section on page 256 to find out if you've won $300!

61

Which Australian golfer lost an eye and an arm in a freak accident involving a plane propellor?

A: Kel Nagle
B: Jack Newton
C: Bruce Crampton
D: Bruce Devlin

62

An Australian cricketing great and television commentator is Richie who?

A: Lawry
B: Benaud
C: Chappell
D: Grieg

63

The Australian echidna is also known as the spiny what-eater?

A: Ant
B: Bee
C: Crow
D: Dung

64

Which of these Australian states is not named after a person?

A: New South Wales
B: Queensland
C: Tasmania
D: Victoria

65

A 1977 Australian film directed by Bruce Beresford is 'The Getting of what'?

A: Good Grades
B: Money
C: Courage
D: Wisdom

If you would like to use your 50:50 please turn to page 242
Turn to the answer section on page 256 to find out if you've won $300!

66

What are the first names of Australia's famous cricketing Waugh twins?

A: Craig & Glenn
B: Ian & Shane
C: Mark & Steve
D: Merv & Ricky

67

Winning the gold medal in a thrilling finish at the 1988 Seoul Olympics was Australia's Debbie Flintoff-who?

A: Duke
B: King
C: Prince
D: Queen

68

A traditional Australian culinary favourite, and a specialty of Flo Bjelke-Petersen is the what scone?

A: Potato
B: Pumpkin
C: Turnip
D: Horseradish

69

A Nancy Cato novel and subsequent TV mini-series is 'All the Rivers what'?

A: Run
B: Flow
C: Hide
D: Dry Up

70

In 1984, 14-year-old Fiona Coote became the youngest person in Australia to receive what organ transplant?

A: Heart
B: Lung
C: Liver
D: Kidney

If you would like to use your 50:50 please turn to page 242
Turn to the answer section on page 256 to find out if you've won $300!

71

An important milestone in Australian manufacturing history, which was the first car mass-produced in Australia?

A: Holden
B: Volkswagen
C: Morris Minor
D: Ford Prefect

72

A shark with a flattened head and eyes in lateral extensions of it, is a what head shark?

A: File
B: Plane
C: Hammer
D: Chisel

73

In which country were a number of Australians killed in a canyoning disaster in July, 1999?

A: South Africa
B: Switzerland
C: Thailand
D: Italy

74

Which people established a tent embassy in Canberra in 1972?

A: Aboriginals
B: Bush walkers
C: Arabs
D: Environmentalists

75

What is the first name of 500cc motorcycle champion Gardner?

A: Bruce
B: Wayne
C: Robin
D: Peter

If you would like to use your 50:50 please turn to page 242
Turn to the answer section on page 256 to find out if you've won $300!

76

In an internet address, www stands for World Wide what?

- A: Window
- B: Web
- C: Word
- D: Workers

77

The official floral emblem of Australia is which species of wattle?

- A: Golden
- B: Silver
- C: Hairy
- D: Cootamundra

78

In 1981, the first Australian golfer to win the US Open was David who?

- A: Ogle
- B: Norman
- C: Graham
- D: Boon

79

What is the form of gambling referred to in the title of the Frank Hardy novel 'The Four-Legged Lottery'?

- A: Horse racing
- B: Pokies
- C: Scratchies
- D: Two-up

80

Which rock musician stood as a Nuclear Disarmament Party Candidate for the Senate in 1984?

- A: Athol Guy
- B: Peter Garrett
- C: Angry Anderson
- D: Jimmy Barnes

If you would like to use your 50:50 please turn to page 242
Turn to the answer section on page 256 to find out if you've won $300!

81

What is the study and investigation of family lines of descent?

A: Genealogy
B: Gerontology
C: Genetics
D: Genome project

82

What name was given to the cyclone which hit Darwin on Christmas morning, 1974?

A: Tracy
B: Cindy
C: Kylie
D: Emmylou

83

The day on which an important operation is to begin or a change to take effect is known as a what letter day?

A: D-Day
B: X-Day
C: P-Day
D: G-Day

84

What is the Rugby term for a touchdown?

A: Attempt
B: Effort
C: Try
D: Eye Gouge

85

What does it mean when a written phrase is put 'in parenthesis'?

A: It is enclosed in brackets
B: It is put in inverted commas
C: It ends with a question mark
D: It is put in code

If you would like to use your 50:50 please turn to page 242
Turn to the answer section on page 256 to find out if you've won $300!

86

What is a cauldron?

- A: Small boat
- B: Boiling pot
- C: Carriage
- D: Prayer

87

How many oars are used to propel a gondola?

- A: One
- B: Two
- C: Three
- D: Four

88

Which English railway station has a fictional bear named after it?

- A: Waterloo
- B: King's Cross
- C: Paddington
- D: Euston

89

Which Scottish town is known as the home of golf?

- A: St Davids
- B: St Andrews
- C: St Patricks
- D: St Georges

90

Which sign of the zodiac is represented by twins?

- A: Taurus
- B: Gemini
- C: Aries
- D: Libra

If you would like to use your 50:50 please turn to page 242
Turn to the answer section on page 256 to find out if you've won $300!

91

What did King Camp Gillette invent?

- A: Caravan
- B: Steam iron
- C: Toothbrush
- D: Safety razor

92

Winner of the 1991 British Open was Australian golfer Ian Baker-who?

- A: Parrot
- B: Nightingale
- C: Crow
- D: Finch

93

A common Australian plant that can provide an essential oil is the what-tree?

- A: Cocoa
- B: Coffee
- C: Tea
- D: Milo

94

Frankie J Holden fronted Australian rock band Ol' what?

- A: 33
- B: 45
- C: 55
- D: Man River

If you would like to use your 50:50 please turn to page 242
Turn to the answer section on page 256 to find out if you've won $300!

50:50

15	$1 MILLION
14	$500,000
13	$250,000
12	$125,000
11	$64,000
10	$32,000
9	$16,000
8	$8,000
7	$4,000
6	$2,000
5	$1,000
4 ◆	$500
3 ◆	$300
2 ◆	$200
1 ◆	$100

4 ◆ $500

1

Who married Prince Rainier of Monaco in 1956?

- A: Marilyn Monroe
- B: Grace Kelly
- C: Ava Gardner
- D: Judy Garland

2

What was the name of Napoleon Bonaparte's first empress?

- A: Claudette
- B: Marie Antoinette
- C: Emma
- D: Josephine

3

Who is Shirley MacLaine's famous film star brother?

- A: Jack Nicholson
- B: Warren Beatty
- C: Gene Hackman
- D: Paul Newman

4

What was Tony Nelson's job in the 1960s sitcom 'I Dream of Jeannie'?

- A: Airline pilot
- B: Fireman
- C: Astronaut
- D: Doctor

5

Which fish has the kinds John, silver and mirror?

- A: Whiting
- B: Trevally
- C: Trout
- D: Dory

If you would like to use your 50:50 please turn to page 243
Turn to the answer section on page 257 to find out if you've won $500!

6

Who played fictional movie star Anna Scott in the film 'Notting Hill'?

- A: Andie MacDowell
- B: Sandra Bullock
- C: Julia Roberts
- D: Cameron Diaz

7

On the market for many years, which brand of tea features a swagman and a kangaroo?

- A: Billy Tea
- B: Bushell's
- C: Dilmah
- D: Kinkara

8

In which city is the permanent home of the Bolshoi Ballet?

- A: Moscow
- B: New York
- C: Milan
- D: Paris

9

What was the first name of President Mitterand of France?

- A: Jacques
- B: Charles
- C: Francois
- D: Edouard

10

Woolloomooloo and Woollahra are suburbs of which Australian capital city?

- A: Melbourne
- B: Sydney
- C: Brisbane
- D: Perth

If you would like to use your 50:50 please turn to page 243
Turn to the answer section on page 257 to find out if you've won $500!

11

The Queensland blue is a variety of which vegetable?

- A: Turnip
- B: Artichoke
- C: Cabbage
- D: Pumpkin

12

How many Academy Awards did the 1997 film 'Titanic' receive?

- A: 1
- B: 2
- C: 4
- D: 11

13

What word describes a person who illegally gains access to private computer systems using a PC?

- A: Surfer
- B: Hacker
- C: Looker
- D: Tracker

14

In which Australian capital city are the Eagle Farm and Doomben racecourses?

- A: Brisbane
- B: Perth
- C: Sydney
- D: Adelaide

15

Which tree has the kinds, hoop, huon and radiata?

- A: Gum
- B: Pine
- C: Laurel
- D: Ash

If you would like to use your 50:50 please turn to page 243
Turn to the answer section on page 257 to find out if you've won $500!

16

In which New South Wales town did Don Bradman begin his cricketing career?

- A: Cootamundra
- B: Mittagong
- C: Bowral
- D: Picton

17

Which commercially important group of crustacea has the kinds banana, tiger and king?

- A: Crayfish
- B: Crabs
- C: Lobsters
- D: Prawns

18

Geoffrey Rush won a Best Actor Oscar for his role in which film?

- A: Shine
- B: The Piano
- C: Babe
- D: Elizabeth

19

Introduced to Australia by Italian immigrants, bocce is similar to which other game?

- A: Bowls
- B: Basketball
- C: Badminton
- D: Squash

20

In which part of the world is the 'limbo' a local dance?

- A: Hawaii
- B: East Africa
- C: West Indies
- D: Indonesia

If you would like to use your 50:50 please turn to page 243
Turn to the answer section on page 257 to find out if you've won $500!

21

On 14th July, 1997, in which country did a bridge collapse causing death and injury to Australian competitors in the Maccabiah Games?

A: Israel
B: France
C: South Korea
D: Canada

22

'Home Amongst the Gum Trees' is the theme song of which TV show?

A: Good Medicine
B: Burke's Backyard
C: Getaway
D: Postcards

23

What is the purpose behind what is known as 'the great Australian salute'?

A: Anzac Day gesture
B: Honour the Queen
C: Acknowledge a sporting triumph
D: Brush flies off one's face

24

Australian Ralph Sarich is famous for developing the orbital combustion what?

A: Clothes hoist
B: Engine
C: Satellite
D: Wood heater

25

What gives the Greek spirit ouzo its flavour?

A: Aubergine
B: Cheese
C: Tobacco
D: Aniseed

If you would like to use your 50:50 please turn to page 243
Turn to the answer section on page 257 to find out if you've won $500!

26

The Queensland groper is one of the largest known what, found in Australian waters?

A: Giant clam
B: Catamaran
C: Glass-bottom boat
D: Fish

27

What animal's name is given to a vote which automatically follows the order in which candidates are listed on the ballot paper?

A: Donkey
B: Drongo
C: Goose
D: Bunny

28

What was Madonna's first single to enter the Australian singles chart?

A: Holiday
B: Vogue
C: Frozen
D: Erotica

29

The aboriginal actor who appeared in 'Crocodile Dundee II' is Ernie who?

A: Sigley
B: Dingo
C: Wise
D: Hogan

30

Which sign of the zodiac is represented by a ram?

A: Aquarius
B: Capricorn
C: Taurus
D: Aries

If you would like to use your 50:50 please turn to page 243
Turn to the answer section on page 257 to find out if you've won $500!

31

Who was the first Australian to win the women's singles title at Wimbledon?

A: Billie Jean King
B: Alice Marble
C: Betty Nuthall
D: Margaret Court

32

Which governor general dismissed the Commonwealth Labor government led by Gough Whitlam in 1975?

A: Kerr
B: Hasluck
C: Stephen
D: Cowen

33

The Court of Disputed Returns deals with disputes about which matters?

A: Customs
B: Migration
C: Prisons
D: Elections

34

Causing much controversy, the book purportedly written by Ukrainian Australian Helen Demidenko is titled 'The Hand That Signed the what'?

A: Autograph Book
B: Petition
C: Cheque
D: Paper

35

Representing Australia in Rugby Union, what is the surname of the brothers Mark, Glen and Gary?

A: Farmer
B: Sands
C: Ella
D: Mundine

If you would like to use your 50:50 please turn to page 243
Turn to the answer section on page 257 to find out if you've won $500!

36

In the Bible, who was killed by Cain?

A: Noah
B: Aaron
C: Abel
D: Moses

37

Da Nang was a key city during which war?

A: Korean
B: Boer
C: Crimean
D: Vietnam

38

John, Johannesburg and Jupiter are all names, but what type of word is a 'name'?

A: Proper noun
B: Pronoun
C: Preposition
D: Adjective

39

What nationality was shared by the composers Vivaldi and Verdi?

A: Swedish
B: Italian
C: French
D: German

40

The abbreviation CPI literally stands for Consumer Price what?

A: Index
B: Institute
C: Inspector
D: Investment

If you would like to use your 50:50 please turn to page 243
Turn to the answer section on page 257 to find out if you've won $500!

41

The first known European to have set foot on the west coast of Australia was Dutch sea captain Dirck who?

A: Hartog
B: Tasman
C: Dampier
D: Flinders

42

Who is the wife of former prime minister Malcolm Fraser?

A: Sonia
B: Zara
C: Gwen
D: Tammy

43

A famous Nevil Shute novel and Hollywood film starring Gregory Peck and Ava Gardner is 'On the what'?

A: Beach
B: Boardwalk
C: Bounty
D: Buses

44

Which of these colours does not appear on the Italian flag?

A: Red
B: Grey
C: Green
D: White

45

Mildura is a Victorian town on which river?

A: Yarra
B: Torrens
C: Clarence
D: Murray

If you would like to use your 50:50 please turn to page 243
Turn to the answer section on page 257 to find out if you've won $500!

46

Near which New South Wales town is the Western Plains Zoo the best known tourist attraction?

- A: Dubbo
- B: Culcairn
- C: Canowindra
- D: Young

47

In colloquial language, to make an all-out effort is to go for which person?

- A: The Doctor
- B: The Dentist
- C: The Lawyer
- D: The Undertaker

48

Who or what is a vegan?

- A: Native of Las Vegas
- B: Alien
- C: Strict vegetarian
- D: Plant

49

In its final stages, which river bisects the city of Hobart?

- A: Parramatta
- B: Swan
- C: Derwent
- D: Tamar

50

Specialising in Russian productions, notably the Moscow Circus and the Bolshoi Ballet, is show-business entrepreneur Michael who?

- A: Evans
- B: Edgley
- C: Miller
- D: Williamson

If you would like to use your 50:50 please turn to page 243
Turn to the answer section on page 257 to find out if you've won $500!

4 ◆ $500

51

What venemous creature is a copperhead?

A: Spider
B: Snake
C: Scorpion
D: Jellyfish

52

In Australian politics, the Coalition traditionally consists of the Liberals and which other party?

A: Australian Labor Party
B: Australian Democrats
C: National Party
D: One Nation

53

Which Australian tennis player won two successive US Open men's singles titles in the 1990s?

A: Pat Cash
B: Mark Philippoussis
C: Patrick Rafter
D: Mark Woodforde

54

Which popular hobby is also known as 'ornithology'?

A: Dressmaking
B: Birdwatching
C: Seafishing
D: Clockwatching

55

Actress Rachel Ward is married to which Australian actor?

A: Tony Martin
B: Bryan Brown
C: Peter Phelps
D: Jack Thompson

If you would like to use your 50:50 please turn to page 243
Turn to the answer section on page 257 to find out if you've won $500!

56

Western Australia's first AFL club was the West Coast what?

A: Eagles
B: Beagles
C: Beetles
D: Bagels

57

What was the title of Shakin' Stevens' hit which topped the charts in 1981?

A: Yellow Window
B: Green Door
C: Blue Room
D: Red Roof

58

An Australian pop group with the hit songs 'Cruel' and 'Last to Know' is Human what?

A: Beings
B: Error
C: Nature
D: Rights

59

What is Frasier's surname in the TV sitcom?

A: Peacock
B: Crane
C: Stork
D: Heron

60

What is the nickname of former Australian cricket captain Mark Taylor?

A: Fatty
B: Piggy
C: Chubby
D: Tubby

If you would like to use your 50:50 please turn to page 243
Turn to the answer section on page 257 to find out if you've won $500!

4 ◆ $500

61

The comedian 'behind the bar' on TV's AFL version of 'The Footy Show' is Trevor who?

- A: Powerade
- B: Marmalade
- C: Lemonade
- D: Gatorade

62

In Australian vernacular, something useless or broken is said to be what plant?

- A: Camellia
- B: Eucalyptus
- C: Cactus
- D: Gladiolius

63

Which Australian city is the main setting for the hit movie 'Mission Impossible 2'?

- A: Brisbane
- B: Perth
- C: Sydney
- D: Wonthaggi

64

An enigmatic Australian actor and personality was Frank who?

- A: Fring
- B: Ring
- C: Thing
- D: Thring

65

The largest of its kind in Australia, the voluntary welfare organisation established in Sydney in 1922 is the what Family?

- A: Jones
- B: Brown
- C: Clark
- D: Smith

If you would like to use your 50:50 please turn to page 243
Turn to the answer section on page 257 to find out if you've won $500!

66

In which area of insurance does one arrange 'gap' cover?

A: Life
B: Accident
C: Public Liability
D: Medical

67

Sydney International Airport is named after which great Australian aviator?

A: Bert Hinkler
B: Charles Kingsford Smith
C: Keith Smith
D: Ross Smith

68

The 'Kingswood' is an Australian car made by which company?

A: Ford
B: Holden
C: Mazda
D: Toyota

69

Which food is made from ground almonds, sugar and egg whites?

A: Marzipan
B: Marmite
C: Marjoram
D: Marmalade

70

What is the Friday before Easter Sunday called?

A: Holy Friday
B: Maundy Friday
C: Good Friday
D: First Friday

If you would like to use your 50:50 please turn to page 243
Turn to the answer section on page 257 to find out if you've won $500!

4 ◆ $500

71

Big Island is a Tasmanian description of which neighbour?

A: Flinders Island
B: King Island
C: Cape Barren Island
D: Mainland Australia

72

In Aussie rhyming slang, a dollar is a 'what scholar'?

A: Cambridge
B: Harvard
C: Oxford
D: Yale

73

Which of these can you find in the NSW city of Tamworth?

A: Big Orange
B: Big Merino
C: Big Lobster
D: Big Guitar

74

Which Australian sports stadium is known simply as The G?

A: Bruce Stadium
B: The Gabba
C: Melbourne Cricket Ground
D: Sydney Cricket Ground

75

Which character was played by Diana Rigg in the TV series 'The Avengers'?

A: Tara King
B: Cathy Gale
C: Purdey
D: Emma Peel

If you would like to use your 50:50 please turn to page 243
Turn to the answer section on page 257 to find out if you've won $500!

76

In mainly what language is the Australian newspaper 'Il Globo' published?

A: Arabic
B: English
C: Vietnamese
D: Italian

77

Called the 'Golden Girl' of country music is Australian singer/songwriter Gina who?

A: Chambers
B: Jeffreys
C: Riley
D: Dusty

78

An Australian champion marathon runner is Steve who?

A: Moneghetti
B: Martin-Ondieki
C: Capobianco
D: De Castella

79

Which American sitcom starred Michael J Fox as the Deputy Mayor of New York City?

A: Caroline in the City
B: Sex and the City
C: Seinfeld
D: Spin City

80

Soon passing into folklore, whose last words were 'Such is life'?

A: Ned Kelly
B: Breaker Morant
C: Ronald Ryan
D: Squizzy Taylor

If you would like to use your 50:50 please turn to page 243
Turn to the answer section on page 257 to find out if you've won $500!

81

The 61-year-old potato farmer who won the first Sydney-to-Melbourne ultra marathon in 1983 was Cliff who?

- A: Old
- B: Otway
- C: Young
- D: Richard

82

What was traditionally thrown down by a knight issuing a challenge?

- A: Lance
- B: Shield
- C: Helmet
- D: Gauntlet

83

A famous landmark in the Northern Territory is what Gorge?

- A: Anne
- B: Elizabeth
- C: Katherine
- D: Margaret

84

What sort of race is Australia's Cox Plate?

- A: Foot race
- B: Horse race
- C: Motor race
- D: Motorcycle race

85

What is the nickname of Australia's national Rugby Union team?

- A: Kangaroos
- B: Koalas
- C: Wallabies
- D: Wombats

If you would like to use your 50:50 please turn to page 243
Turn to the answer section on page 257 to find out if you've won $500!

86

Which river is also the name of a member of a tribe of legendary female warriors?

A: Thames
B: Nile
C: Amazon
D: Rhine

87

What disaster occurred in the Sydney suburb of Granville in 1977?

A: Bushfire
B: Gas explosion
C: Plane crash
D: Train wreck

88

What was the name of the Spanish waiter in the TV sitcom 'Fawlty Towers'?

A: Pedro
B: Alfonso
C: Manuel
D: Javier

89

Who was the lead singer for Australian band Sherbet?

A: John Farnham
B: Russell Hitchcock
C: Nick Cave
D: Daryl Braithwaite

90

In Sydney, what is a southerly buster?

A: Hailstorm
B: Bus service
C: Cool wind
D: Local boxer

If you would like to use your 50:50 please turn to page 243
Turn to the answer section on page 257 to find out if you've won $500!

15 $1 MILLION

14 $500,000

13 $250,000

12 $125,000

11 $64,000

10 $32,000

9 $16,000

8 $8,000

7 $4,000

6 $2,000

5 ◆ $1,000

4 ◆ $500

3 ◆ $300

2 ◆ $200

1 ◆ $100

5 ◆ $1,000

1

What is the longest river in Italy?

A: Po
B: Laa-Laa
C: Dipsy
D: Tinky Winky

2

In knitting, what is the name of the stitch made by doing a plain stitch backwards?

A: Purl
B: Curl
C: Whurl
D: Gurl

3

A Mancunian is a native of which English city?

A: Birmingham
B: Liverpool
C: Manchester
D: London

4

Which day occurs first in an Australian calendar year?

A: Boxing Day
B: Easter Sunday
C: Queen's Birthday
D: Melbourne Cup Day

5

In July, 1997, 18 people were killed in a landslide in what Snowy Mountains resort?

A: Smiggins Holes
B: Thredbo
C: Perisher
D: Mt.Hotham

If you would like to use your 50:50 please turn to page 245
Turn to the answer section on page 257 to find out if you've won $1,000!

6

Who quit the Spice Girls in 1998?

- A: Geri
- B: Victoria
- C: Emma
- D: Mel C

7

In colloquial language, to depart hastily is to shoot through like a Bondi what?

- A: Bus
- B: Tram
- C: Train
- D: Taxi

8

What name is usually given to the International Criminal Police Organisation?

- A: The Professionals
- B: Scotland Yard
- C: Interpol
- D: Flying Squad

9

How many players take the field in an Australian Rules football team?

- A: 18
- B: 11
- C: 15
- D: 13

10

Which state is home to over 40% of Australia's vineyards?

- A: New South Wales
- B: South Australia
- C: Tasmania
- D: Western Australia

If you would like to use your 50:50 please turn to page 245
Turn to the answer section on page 257 to find out if you've won $1,000!

5 ◆ $1,000

11

Visiting Australia in 1891 was which great French actress known as 'The Divine Sarah'?

A: Terru
B: Churchill
C: Siddons
D: Bernhardt

12

By what simple name is the monsoon season known in the Northern Territory?

A: The Deluge
B: The Fall
C: The Wash
D: The Wet

13

A legendary name in television news reading is Sir Eric who?

A: Henderson
B: Naylor
C: Pearce
D: Waley

14

The platypus and which bird are the faunal emblems of NSW?

A: Kookaburra
B: Indian mynah
C: Crow
D: Budgerigar

15

In which small Victorian town was Ned Kelly captured in June, 1880?

A: Glenrowan
B: Glen Innes
C: Glenelg
D: Glengarry

If you would like to use your 50:50 please turn to page 245
Turn to the answer section on page 257 to find out if you've won $1,000!

16

Of what is orange pekoe a variety?

A: Dog
B: Tea
C: Apple
D: Duck

17

What is myopia?

A: Short-sightedness
B: Deafness
C: Baldness
D: Tooth decay

18

In London, which river is crossed by the Tower Bridge?

A: Severn
B: Thames
C: Nile
D: Seine

19

Which country was once ruled by tsars?

A: Ireland
B: Japan
C: Russia
D: China

20

Highly prized as food, what type of marine creature is a blue swimmer?

A: Fish
B: Oyster
C: Crab
D: Scallop

If you would like to use your 50:50 please turn to page 245
Turn to the answer section on page 257 to find out if you've won $1,000!

5 ◆ $1,000

21

Which Australian swimming champion won three gold medals at the 1972 Munich Olympics?

A: Beverley Whitfield
B: Shane Gould
C: Lorraine Crapp
D: Michelle Ford

22

Who sang about being a 'Private Dancer' in the 1984 singles chart?

A: Belinda Carlisle
B: Tina Turner
C: Whitney Houston
D: Madonna

23

In which Australian state is the district known as Gippsland?

A: Queensland
B: Western Australia
C: Victoria
D: Tasmania

24

What is the more common name for bruising around one's ocular apparatus, resulting from a blow?

A: Black eye
B: Love bite
C: Cauliflower ear
D: Fat lip

25

What is the name of the enclosed platform in a church from which a sermon is delivered?

A: Pulpit
B: Nave
C: Altar
D: Transept

If you would like to use your 50:50 please turn to page 245
Turn to the answer section on page 257 to find out if you've won $1,000!

5 ◆ $1,000

26

Diana Ross topped the singles charts in 1986 with her 'Chain . . . ' what?

- A: Letter
- B: Gang
- C: Mail
- D: Reaction

27

What kind of creature is a flying fox?

- A: Possum
- B: Lizard
- C: Bat
- D: Bird

28

In the Old Testament, an angel with a flaming sword prevented Adam and Eve returning to which place?

- A: Eden
- B: Land of Nod
- C: Sodom
- D: Gomorrah

29

Which hero was the subject of a Disney animated feature film in 1997?

- A: Ulysses
- B: Hercules
- C: Perseus
- D: Achilles

30

To be controlled by a brutal military regime is to be under the jack what?

- A: Knife
- B: Hammer
- C: O'-lantern
- D: Boot

If you would like to use your 50:50 please turn to page 245
Turn to the answer section on page 257 to find out if you've won $1,000!

31

Which bird's name means 'two under par' in golf?

- A: Duck
- B: Sparrow
- C: Eagle
- D: Vulture

32

Which actor was pursued by a crop-dusting aeroplane in the Hitchcock film 'North by Northwest'?

- A: John Wayne
- B: Cary Grant
- C: Paul Newman
- D: Bob Hope

33

Juan Antonio Samaranch became President of which organisation in 1980?

- A: OPEC
- B: RSPCA
- C: IOC
- D: ASIO

34

In which part of the world did calypso music originate?

- A: Japan
- B: Australia
- C: West Indies
- D: South Pacific

35

In 1980, who recorded 'Shaddap You Face', one of the largest-selling Australian singles ever?

- A: Joe Dolce
- B: Nino Culotta
- C: Carlo Catani
- D: Raffaello Carboni

If you would like to use your 50:50 please turn to page 245
Turn to the answer section on page 257 to find out if you've won $1,000!

36

A place of work where all employees must belong to an agreed trade union is called a closed what?

- A: Office
- B: Site
- C: Factory
- D: Shop

37

The Queensland or bopple nut are alternative names for which native nut?

- A: Macadamia
- B: Geebung
- C: Almond
- D: Walnut

38

In which country was businessman Alan Bond born in 1938?

- A: England
- B: USA
- C: New Zealand
- D: South Africa

39

Who are Athos, Porthos and Aramis?

- A: Three Stooges
- B: Three Wise Men
- C: Marx Brothers
- D: Three Musketeers

40

In the 1983 horror film 'Christine', what was Christine?

- A: Car
- B: Lamppost
- C: Hamburger
- D: Tortoise

If you would like to use your 50:50 please turn to page 245
Turn to the answer section on page 257 to find out if you've won $1,000!

41

In population, which is the third largest city in Australia?

- A: Canberra
- B: Newcastle
- C: Perth
- D: Brisbane

42

How many sides has the Australian 50-cent piece?

- A: 6
- B: 8
- C: 10
- D: 12

43

Which North American animal has a distinctive black mask and a striped tail?

- A: Grizzly bear
- B: Bald eagle
- C: Coyote
- D: Raccoon

44

The longest novel ever published in Australia is Xavier Herbert's 'Poor Fellow My what'?

- A: Mate
- B: Father
- C: Neighbour
- D: Country

45

Who played the title role in Jane Campion's film 'The Portrait of a Lady'?

- A: Frances O'Connor
- B: Susie Porter
- C: Toni Collette
- D: Nicole Kidman

If you would like to use your 50:50 please turn to page 245
Turn to the answer section on page 257 to find out if you've won $1,000!

46

Which word means to debase by mixing with something inferior?

- A: Adulate
- B: Adjudicate
- C: Advocate
- D: Adulterate

47

Who won an Oscar for 'The Godfather' but refused to accept it?

- A: Marlon Brando
- B: Al Pacino
- C: Francis Ford Coppola
- D: Diane Keaton

48

What was the 1951 treaty signed by Australia, New Zealand and the United States to counter aggression in the Pacific?

- A: Anzac
- B: Anzus
- C: Asean
- D: Usanz

49

Which of these Australian hit songs was by Aboriginal band Yothu Yindi?

- A: Treat Me Good
- B: Treaty
- C: Truly, Madly, Deeply
- D: Try Whistling This

50

The Australian bird famous for its mimicry is the what bird?

- A: Harp
- B: Lute
- C: Lyre
- D: Banjo

If you would like to use your 50:50 please turn to page 245
Turn to the answer section on page 257 to find out if you've won $1,000!

51

In what month is the AFL Grand Final traditionally played?

A: March
B: July
C: September
D: December

52

What name is given to the high-speed trains of Japan?

A: Rocket trains
B: Bullet trains
C: Greyhound trains
D: Eagle trains

53

The acronym of which Australian company is also a unit for measuring electric current?

A: AMP
B: ANZ
C: GIO
D: TAB

54

What is the Earth's only natural satellite?

A: Moon
B: Pluto
C: Krypton
D: Sun

55

Northern Territory's Arnhem Land is separated from Queensland's Cape York Peninsula by which body of water?

A: Great Australian Bight
B: Bass Strait
C: Gulf of Carpentaria
D: Joseph Bonaparte Gulf

If you would like to use your 50:50 please turn to page 245
Turn to the answer section on page 257 to find out if you've won $1,000!

56

Which American presented a Gold Logie to Bert Newton, who responded with the now infamous line 'I like the boy'?

- A: Muhammad Ali
- B: George Burns
- C: Macaulay Culkin
- D: Phyllis Diller

57

Which city hosted the 1956 Summer Olympic Games?

- A: Melbourne
- B: Manchester
- C: Milan
- D: Miami

58

A large Australian food-fish is the what cod?

- A: Murrumbidgee
- B: Murray
- C: Lachlan
- D: Hawkesbury

59

What is the Australian horse race 'that stops the nation'?

- A: Adelaide Cup
- B: Melbourne Cup
- C: Sydney Cup
- D: Perth Cup

60

Which of these soups traditionally contains fish?

- A: Minestrone
- B: Mulligatawny
- C: Chowder
- D: Cock-a-leekie

If you would like to use your 50:50 please turn to page 245
Turn to the answer section on page 257 to find out if you've won $1,000!

61

What is former British Prime Minister Margaret Thatcher's middle name?

- A: Harriet
- B: Hilda
- C: Hyacinth
- D: Helga

62

Which Emperor was defeated by the Duke of Wellington and Marshal Blucher in 1815?

- A: Charles the Bald
- B: Louis the Fat
- C: Napoleon I
- D: Franz Josef II

63

Which 1960 million seller for Elvis Presley was based on the Italian song 'O Sole Mio'?

- A: It's Now or Never
- B: Love Me Tender
- C: Heartbreak Hotel
- D: All Shook Up

64

For what does the second 'A' literally stand in the acronym QANTAS?

- A: Airway
- B: Arterial
- C: Air
- D: Aerial

65

Hydroponics is a term related to which of the following?

- A: Whale song
- B: Plant growing
- C: Sea travel
- D: Humidity measurement

If you would like to use your 50:50 please turn to page 245
Turn to the answer section on page 257 to find out if you've won $1,000!

66

'Salary' is derived from the Latin word for the allowance paid to Roman soldiers to buy what?

- A: Salt
- B: Togas
- C: Leather and hide to repair boots
- D: Chariots

67

What did the U stand for in USSR?

- A: United
- B: Union
- C: Ukraine
- D: Universal

68

Primarily concerned with the preservation of marriage and the family is the Christian organisation the Festival of what?

- A: Heaven
- B: Light
- C: Glory
- D: Angels

69

Uniquely Australian, Federation is a style of what?

- A: Dress
- B: Cookery
- C: Architecture
- D: Furniture

70

Housewife superstar Dame Edna Everage had her origins in which suburb of Melbourne?

- A: Toorak
- B: Kew
- C: Carlton
- D: Moonee Ponds

If you would like to use your 50:50 please turn to page 245
Turn to the answer section on page 257 to find out if you've won $1,000!

71

Who wrote 'Journey to the Centre of the Earth'?

A: Victor Hugo
B: Jules Verne
C: Moliere
D: Gustave Flaubert

72

What was the lowest value note when decimal currency was introduced in February 1966?

A: $1
B: $5
C: $10
D: $20

73

The timber from a eucalypt or deciduous broad-leaved tree as distinct from that of conifers is known by what name?

A: Hardwood
B: Softwood
C: Lightwood
D: Heavywood

74

Which explorer's name is given to a desert pea?

A: Kennedy
B: Eyre
C: Sturt
D: Cook

75

Excluding daylight saving, how many hours is Eastern Standard Time ahead of Western Standard Time?

A: One
B: Two
C: Three
D: Four

If you would like to use your 50:50 please turn to page 245
Turn to the answer section on page 257 to find out if you've won $1,000!

76

To reverse a trend towards excessive foreign ownership of capital assets is to buy back the what?

- A: Farm
- B: Estate
- C: Station
- D: Family jewels

77

Which Australian actor was nominated for an Academy Award for her role in the 1984 film 'A Passage to India'?

- A: Jacki Weaver
- B: Judy Davis
- C: Helen Morse
- D: Toni Collette

78

FIFA is the governing body for which sport?

- A: Tennis
- B: Soccer
- C: Swimming
- D: Athletics

79

Which politician famously danced the macarena with Kerri-Anne Kennerley on TV's 'Midday Show'?

- A: Bob Hawke
- B: Kim Beazley
- C: Peter Costello
- D: John Howard

80

Which Australian rocker had the hit song 'Shout'?

- A: Col Joye
- B: Johnny O'Keefe
- C: Normie Rowe
- D: Jimmy Barnes

If you would like to use your 50:50 please turn to page 245
Turn to the answer section on page 257 to find out if you've won $1,000!

81

Ted Whitten was a champion in which sport?

- A: Australian Rules
- B: Golf
- C: Rugby League
- D: Tennis

82

Which of these was a hit song for Australian rock band Cold Chisel?

- A: Da Nang
- B: Khe Sanh
- C: Dong Hoi
- D: Ho Chi Minh

83

A brand of what common household appliance was named after British scientist Lord Kelvin?

- A: Kettle
- B: Microwave
- C: Refrigerator
- D: Toaster

84

Which NRL team has the aptly-named nickname of the Dragons?

- A: Penrith
- B: Balmain
- C: Cronulla
- D: St George-Illawarra

85

In which sport are Robert Allenby and Stuart Appleby prominent Australians?

- A: Golf
- B: Squash
- C: Swimming
- D: Tennis

If you would like to use your 50:50 please turn to page 245
Turn to the answer section on page 257 to find out if you've won $1,000!

86

What was the name of the winged horse of Greek mythology?

- A: Silver
- B: Bellerophon
- C: Champion
- D: Pegasus

If you would like to use your 50:50 please turn to page 245
Turn to the answer section on page 257 to find out if you've won $1,000!

50:50

15		$1 MILLION
14		$500,000
13		$250,000
12		$125,000
11		$64,000
10		$32,000
9		$16,000
8		$8,000
7		$4,000
6	◆	$2,000
5	◆	$1,000
4	◆	$500
3	◆	$300
2	◆	$200
1	◆	$100

6 ◆ $2,000

1

Which of these films did not star Cher?

- A: Mask
- B: Mermaids
- C: Misery
- D: Moonstruck

2

Which superhero has been portrayed on screen by Michael Keaton, Val Kilmer and George Clooney?

- A: Batman
- B: Spiderman
- C: Captain America
- D: Wonder Woman

3

Which US state is nicknamed the Empire State?

- A: New York
- B: California
- C: Alaska
- D: Texas

4

The Eureka Stockade is the name given to an armed uprising in 1854 by miners at which goldfield?

- A: Ballarat
- B: Hill End
- C: Charters Towers
- D: Kalgoorlie

5

What kind of animal is Nipper, in the famous HMV logo?

- A: Budgerigar
- B: Piranha
- C: Giraffe
- D: Dog

If you would like to use your 50:50 please turn to page 246
Turn to the answer section on page 258 to find out if you've won $2,000!

6

According to the nursery rhyme, who killed Cock Robin?

A: The wren
B: The rook
C: The thrush
D: The sparrow

7

As what did Sir Walter Raleigh become famous?

A: Explorer
B: Bicycle maker
C: Composer
D: Court jester

8

Which former racing driver set up his own international airline?

A: Alain Prost
B: Jackie Stewart
C: Niki Lauda
D: Nigel Mansell

9

On which continent is the country of South Korea?

A: Africa
B: Antarctica
C: South America
D: Asia

10

In which country is the Gallipoli Peninsula?

A: France
B: Turkey
C: Libya
D: Egypt

If you would like to use your 50:50 please turn to page 246
Turn to the answer section on page 258 to find out if you've won $2,000!

11

Which mythological sisters were monstrous creatures with the power to turn a viewer to stone?

- A: Gorgonzola
- B: Bacchante
- C: Furies
- D: Gorgons

12

What is America's theatrical equivalent of the Oscars?

- A: Tims
- B: Tonys
- C: Toms
- D: Trevors

13

Gaelic is a type of what?

- A: Aromatic herb
- B: Celtic language
- C: Swiss cheese
- D: Egyptian writing paper

14

In which sport was Daley Thompson an Olympic champion?

- A: Cycling
- B: Shooting
- C: Athletics
- D: Diving

15

Who played Scarlett O'Hara in the 1939 film 'Gone With The Wind' ?

- A: Vivien Leigh
- B: Olivia De Havilland
- C: Ingrid Bergman
- D: Katharine Hepburn

If you would like to use your 50:50 please turn to page 246
Turn to the answer section on page 258 to find out if you've won $2,000!

16

In 'The X-Files', what is Agent Mulder's first name?

- A: Fox
- B: Hound
- C: Tiger
- D: Wolf

17

Which Shakespeare play features the characters Shylock and Portia?

- A: The Merchant of Venice
- B: Twelfth Night
- C: Titus Andronicus
- D: The Winter's Tale

18

The Nilsson song 'Everybody's Talkin'' became a hit when it featured in which film?

- A: 'Midnight Cowboy'
- B: 'The Graduate'
- C: 'Love Story'
- D: 'Shampoo'

19

What did the Romans call a marketplace or public square?

- A: Curia
- B: Basilica
- C: Forum
- D: Nomen

20

According to Edward Lear, the Owl and the Pussy-Cat went to sea in a boat of which colour?

- A: Sky blue
- B: Pea green
- C: Jet black
- D: Brick red

If you would like to use your 50:50 please turn to page 246
Turn to the answer section on page 258 to find out if you've won $2,000!

21

Which of these cities is built upon a group of islands?

- A: Madrid
- B: Paris
- C: Edinburgh
- D: Venice

22

Who starred opposite Patrick Swayze in the hit 1987 film 'Dirty Dancing'?

- A: Jennifer Grey
- B: Jennifer Beals
- C: Jennifer Tilly
- D: Jennifer Aniston

23

What is the Australian film that stars Jack Thompson and Russell Crowe as father and gay son, respectively?

- A: The Same as Us
- B: Simon and Gus
- C: Some and Us
- D: The Sum of Us

24

How many stripes appear on the flag of the USA?

- A: Two
- B: Three
- C: Thirteen
- D: Fifty

25

Derived from an Aboriginal language, the name Canberra is thought to mean which of the following?

- A: Meeting place
- B: Big noise
- C: Easy life
- D: Club fed

If you would like to use your 50:50 please turn to page 246
Turn to the answer section on page 258 to find out if you've won $2,000!

26

Which lines on a map join places of equal elevation?

- A: Ley lines
- B: Contour lines
- C: Plimsoll lines
- D: Slope lines

27

Peter Allen co-wrote the lyrics to the Oscar winning theme song from which 1981 movie?

- A: Kramer vs Kramer
- B: Chariots of Fire
- C: Gandhi
- D: Arthur

28

Which Australian rock band fronted by Michael Hutchence had the hits 'Need You Tonight' and 'Suicide Blonde'?

- A: Icehouse
- B: INXS
- C: Midnight Oil
- D: Models

29

Which American university shares its name with a kind of lock?

- A: Princeton
- B: Stanford
- C: Yale
- D: Harvard

30

The Henley-on-Todd Regatta is a race run along a dry river bed in which Australian town?

- A: Alice Springs
- B: Burnie
- C: Coober Pedy
- D: Melbourne

If you would like to use your 50:50 please turn to page 246
Turn to the answer section on page 258 to find out if you've won $2,000!

31

Who was Doyle's partner in 'The Professionals'?

A: Shortie
B: Codie
C: Jodie
D: Bodie

32

'I Like It' was a massive hit for 1960s pop group 'Gerry and the . . . ' who?

A: Dreamers
B: Comets
C: Pacemakers
D: Crickets

33

Australian prime minister for much of the 1920s, Stanley Bruce had which middle name?

A: Adelaide
B: Brisbane
C: Perth
D: Melbourne

34

When somebody suffers from mumps, which body parts swell up?

A: Joints
B: Ears
C: Glands
D: Feet

35

Akubra hats are made of the felted fur of which animal?

A: Rabbit
B: Possum
C: Bandicoot
D: Kangaroo

If you would like to use your 50:50 please turn to page 246
Turn to the answer section on page 258 to find out if you've won $2,000!

36

What kind of sausage would you expect to find in a hot dog?

A: Salami
B: Frankfurter
C: Pepperoni
D: Bratwurst

37

What is Perry Mason's occupation in the TV series?

A: Doctor
B: Lawyer
C: Writer
D: Policeman

38

Which group was led by Bryan Ferry in the 1970s?

A: Dire Straits
B: Pink Floyd
C: Roxy Music
D: The Faces

39

Rice that is processed to remove only the husks, with all the bran remaining, is known by which name?

A: Green
B: Wild
C: Brown
D: White

40

Especially in the outback, a hessian covered frame kept moist to preserve perishable foodstuffs is the what safe?

A: Coolangatta
B: Coolgardie
C: Cootamundra
D: Kalgoorlie

If you would like to use your 50:50 please turn to page 246
Turn to the answer section on page 258 to find out if you've won $2,000!

6 ◆ $2,000

41

The headstreams and waters of which river drain half the South American continent?

- A: Orinoco
- B: Paraguay
- C: Amazon
- D: Limpopo

42

What is a mamba?

- A: Dance
- B: Snake
- C: Fruit
- D: Mammal

43

What is a labyrinth?

- A: Maze
- B: Flower
- C: Research centre
- D: Vegetable

44

Whose most famous creation are the Gumnut babies, Bib and Bub, and Snugglepot and Cuddlepie?

- A: Ethel Turner
- B: May Gibbs
- C: Norman Lindsay
- D: Dorothy Well

45

What is at the centre of the Solar System?

- A: Moon
- B: Sun
- C: Earth
- D: Mercury

If you would like to use your 50:50 please turn to page 246
Turn to the answer section on page 258 to find out if you've won $2,000!

46

In which film does Dooley Wilson sing 'As Time Goes By'?

- A: The Maltese Falcon
- B: Casablanca
- C: The African Queen
- D: The Big Sleep

47

What name is given to the top universities in the USA?

- A: Premier League
- B: Laurel League
- C: Super League
- D: Ivy League

48

Who played James Bond in the 1967 film 'You Only Live Twice'?

- A: George Lazenby
- B: Timothy Dalton
- C: Roger Moore
- D: Sean Connery

49

In which sport is the herringbone technique used for going uphill?

- A: Skiing
- B: Rock climbing
- C: Mountain biking
- D: Hang gliding

50

A bonfire was so named because it was originally made from which objects?

- A: Bones
- B: Bonbons
- C: Bonds
- D: Bonnets

If you would like to use your 50:50 please turn to page 246
Turn to the answer section on page 258 to find out if you've won $2,000!

51

Prince William celebrated which birthday on 21st June, 2000?

- A: 16th
- B: 18th
- C: 20th
- D: 21st

52

A bestseller after its first publication in 1981, was 'A Fortunate Life' by Albert who?

- A: Spacey
- B: Facey
- C: Dacey
- D: Casey

53

Which country and western singer is the daughter of Slim Dusty?

- A: Anne Kirkpatrick
- B: Jewel Blanch
- C: Norma Murphy
- D: Ellen Osterfield

54

Which scale is used to test whether garden soil is acid, neutral or alkaline?

- A: Mercalli Scale
- B: Richter Scale
- C: pH Scale
- D: Lime Scale

55

Which of these words describes the force with which an object is impelled?

- A: Gravity
- B: Impetus
- C: Density
- D: Inertia

If you would like to use your 50:50 please turn to page 246
Turn to the answer section on page 258 to find out if you've won $2,000!

56

In 1965, Linda McGill was the first Australian to achieve which feat?

- A: Swim the English Channel
- B: Win an Olympic Medal in skiing
- C: Cross continent in solar-powered vehicle
- D: Deepest undersea dive

57

The brilliant blue butterfly, Papilio ulysses, is a symbol of which tourist resort island off the Queensland coast?

- A: Phillip Island
- B: Rottnest Island
- C: Kangaroo Island
- D: Dunk Island

58

Which Australian prime minister was born in Bordertown, South Australia in 1929?

- A: Whitlam
- B: Fraser
- C: Howard
- D: Hawke

59

'Not a Penny More, Not a Penny Less' was the title of which former British MP's first novel?

- A: Douglas Hurd
- B: Nigel West
- C: Edwina Currie
- D: Jeffrey Archer

60

What is the title of the much-produced Jack Hibberd play subtitled 'A Wedding-Reception Play'?

- A: Dimboola
- B: Tumbarumba
- C: Innamincka
- D: Woop Woop

If you would like to use your 50:50 please turn to page 246
Turn to the answer section on page 258 to find out if you've won $2,000!

61

Who carried the torch into the stadium at the Melbourne Olympics in 1956?

A: Hector Hogan
B: John Landy
C: Herb Elliott
D: Ron Clarke

62

John Doyle and Greig Pickhaver are better known as which Australian comedy duo?

A: Lano and Woodley
B: Merrick and Rosso
C: Roy and HG
D: Scared Weird Little Guys

63

Semaphore is a method of sending signals using what?

A: Flags
B: Mirrors
C: Telegraph
D: Signal lamps

64

The highlight of Corroboree 2000, a celebration of Aboriginal reconciliation, involved a mass walk of over 150,000 people at which Sydney landmark?

A: Centennial Park
B: Harbour Bridge
C: Opera House
D: Luna Park

65

Which of the following was not a member of the first expedition to cross the Blue Mountains?

A: Blaxland
B: Lawson
C: Paterson
D: Wentworth

If you would like to use your 50:50 please turn to page 246
Turn to the answer section on page 258 to find out if you've won $2,000!

66

Which of these groups campaigned for votes for women?

A: Abolitionists
B: Luddites
C: Tolpuddle Martyrs
D: Suffragettes

67

Written under the pseudonym of Nino Culotta, John O'Grady wrote the novel 'They're a Weird what'?

A: Bunch
B: Group
C: Lot
D: Mob

68

Also called the giant perch, which fish is native to Australia?

A: Barracuda
B: Barramundi
C: John Dory
D: Barry McKenzie

69

Which artistic movement was founded by Georges Braque and Pablo Picasso?

A: Triangulism
B: Cubism
C: Pentagonism
D: Octagonism

70

A 1974 Peter Weir film is 'The Cars That Ate where'?

A: London
B: New York
C: Paris
D: Dubbo

If you would like to use your 50:50 please turn to page 246
Turn to the answer section on page 258 to find out if you've won $2,000!

71

What fictitious place is the setting for the TV series 'SeaChange'?

- A: Cockle Harbour
- B: Oyster Cove
- C: Pearl Bay
- D: Shell Beach

72

For what does the letter S stand in ASIO?

- A: Scientific
- B: Secondary
- C: Security
- D: Service

73

Australia's national flag is also called the what colour Ensign?

- A: Blue
- B: Red
- C: White
- D: Green & Gold

74

In 1967, a national referendum was held to include which people in the census of Australian citizens?

- A: Aborigines
- B: Migrants
- C: Women
- D: New Zealanders

If you would like to use your 50:50 please turn to page 246
Turn to the answer section on page 258 to find out if you've won $2,000!

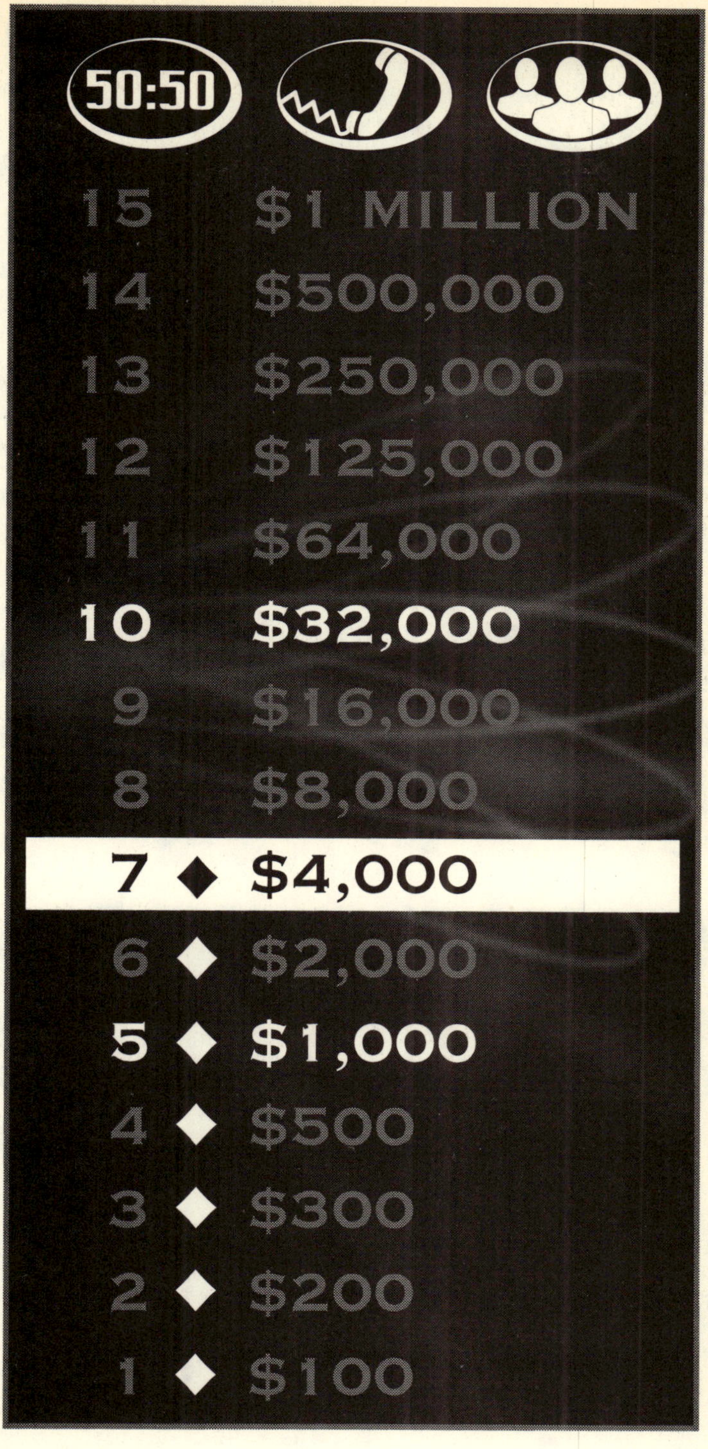

50:50
15 $1 MILLION
14 $500,000
13 $250,000
12 $125,000
11 $64,000
10 $32,000
9 $16,000
8 $8,000
7 ◆ $4,000
6 ◆ $2,000
5 ◆ $1,000
4 ◆ $500
3 ◆ $300
2 ◆ $200
1 ◆ $100

7 ◆ $4,000

1

Which country features a bird of paradise on its national flag?

- A: Papua New Guinea
- B: Indonesia
- C: Thailand
- D: Sri Lanka

2

What is a yashmak?

- A: Veil
- B: Bracelet
- C: Prayer mat
- D: Belt

3

Which of these hit songs was by Australian group The Easybeats?

- A: Eagle Rock
- B: Friday on My Mind
- C: She's My Baby
- D: Yellow River

4

Racehorse trainer Gai Waterhouse is the daughter of which great Australian racehorse trainer?

- A: Bart Cummings
- B: Colin Hayes
- C: T J Smith
- D: Tommy Woodcock

5

Which island is also known as Great Sandy Island?

- A: Kangaroo
- B: Lizard
- C: Fraser
- D: Thursday

If you would like to use your 50:50 please turn to page 247
Turn to the answer section on page 258 to find out if you've won $4,000!

6

In 1950s Australia, what was the female equivalent of a bodgie?

- A: Widgie
- B: Widgeon
- C: Gidget
- D: Gadget

7

Mount Kosciuszko is located in which mountain range?

- A: Flinders Ranges
- B: Grampians
- C: Macdonnell Ranges
- D: Snowy Mountains

8

Alexander Dumas wrote a play titled 'Lady of the what flowers'?

- A: Lilacs
- B: Petunias
- C: Daffodils
- D: Camelias

9

In the sitcom 'Are You Being Served?', whose catchphrase was 'I'm Free'?

- A: Mr Lucas
- B: Captain Peacock
- C: Mrs Slocombe
- D: Mr Humphries

10

The Albert's lyrebird was named after what 19th century historical figure?

- A: Prince Albert
- B: Albert Einstein
- C: Albert I
- D: Albert of Moravia

If you would like to use your 50:50 please turn to page 247
Turn to the answer section on page 258 to find out if you've won $4,000!

11

Sydney won the right to host the 2000 Olympics after defeating which city by just two votes?

- A: Beijing
- B: Istanbul
- C: Manchester
- D: Toronto

12

From 1990, which best-selling novelist turned her attention to publishing a series of historical novels set in ancient Rome?

- A: Colleen McCullough
- B: Patricia Cornwell
- C: Sara Paretsky
- D: Ruth Rendell

13

What might be divided into stanzas?

- A: Land
- B: Time
- C: Poetry
- D: Food

14

What is the main opera house of New York City?

- A: The Metropolitan
- B: The Grand
- C: The Palladium
- D: The Odeon

15

Peter Carey's 1997 award-winning novel bears the title 'Jack who'?

- A: Maggs
- B: Sprat
- C: Thompson
- D: Kennedy

If you would like to use your 50:50 please turn to page 247
Turn to the answer section on page 258 to find out if you've won $4,000!

16

What were Bill Oddie, Graeme Garden and Tim Brooke-Taylor better known as in a TV comedy series?

- A: The Goodies
- B: The A-Team
- C: The Three Stooges
- D: The Young Ones

17

Chapatis come from the cuisine of which country?

- A: China
- B: Italy
- C: France
- D: India

18

Which city gives its name to the French national anthem?

- A: Marseilles
- B: Paris
- C: Lyon
- D: Calais

19

Which New England state is the title of an award-winning song written by the Gibb brothers in the late 60's?

- A: New Hampshire
- B: Connecticut
- C: Vermont
- D: Massachusetts

20

Who played the title role in the epic film 'Lawrence of Arabia'?

- A: Richard Harris
- B: Alec Guinness
- C: Richard Attenborough
- D: Peter O'Toole

If you would like to use your 50:50 please turn to page 247
Turn to the answer section on page 258 to find out if you've won $4,000!

21

From 1964 to 1981, Sir Garfield Barwick was the Chief Justice of which Court?

- A: High
- B: Family
- C: Equity
- D: Land and environment

22

In which city could you visit the famous Topkapi Palace?

- A: Istanbul
- B: Rome
- C: Toronto
- D: Sydney

23

When eaten, which part of a cow is known as tripe?

- A: Tongue
- B: Leg
- C: Neck
- D: Stomach lining

24

Which Latin word is also an everyday English word for a puzzle?

- A: Conundrum
- B: Perplexus
- C: Dubius
- D: Enigma

25

In which sport would 'spoons', 'paternosters' and 'lures' be used?

- A: Golf
- B: Sailing
- C: Clay pigeon shooting
- D: Fishing

If you would like to use your 50:50 please turn to page 247
Turn to the answer section on page 258 to find out if you've won $4,000!

26

What name is given to a symbol on a VDU screen of a facility available for selection?

A: Icon
B: Window
C: Cursor
D: Port

27

The second longest river in Europe, the Danube rises in which forest?

A: Black
B: New
C: Forest of Arden
D: Sherwood

28

Which country was called Siam until 1939?

A: Burma
B: Thailand
C: Vietnam
D: Taiwan

29

Topping bestseller lists in 2000, was what book about Australia by travel writer Bill Bryson?

A: Land of the Long Weekend
B: Antipodean Adventure
C: Down Under
D: Ozzie

30

In which field did John Constable become famous?

A: Art
B: Fashion
C: Literature
D: Politics

If you would like to use your 50:50 please turn to page 247
Turn to the answer section on page 258 to find out if you've won $4,000!

31

A calicivirus was introduced to Australia in the mid-1990s as a biological control for which pest?

A: Feral cats
B: Deer
C: Fox
D: Rabbits

32

On which continent are the five 'Great Lakes'?

A: Europe
B: Australia
C: Africa
D: North America

33

Socrates was a famous philosopher in which civilisation?

A: Roman
B: Greek
C: Egyptian
D: Chinese

34

Which car became known as a 'Tin Lizzie'?

A: Austin 7
B: Model T Ford
C: Volkswagen Beetle
D: Mini

35

In early 1998, an American tourist couple mysteriously disappeared after being left behind where?

A: Great Barrier Reef
B: Hanging Rock
C: Uluru
D: New Zealand

If you would like to use your 50:50 please turn to page 247
Turn to the answer section on page 258 to find out if you've won $4,000!

36

Between 1577 and 1580, who captained a ship called the Golden Hind?

- A: Francis Drake
- B: Christopher Columbus
- C: Roald Amundsen
- D: Charles Darwin

37

In 1770, Captain Cook named which waterway Stingray Harbour?

- A: Port Jackson
- B: Jervis Bay
- C: Botany Bay
- D: Broken Bay

38

Which Australian scientist shared a Nobel Prize for his part in developing penicillin?

- A: Florey
- B: Oliphant
- C: Eccles
- D: Gregg

39

Clunes was the site of the first major discovery of what valuable commodity in Victoria in July, 1851?

- A: Diamonds
- B: Gold
- C: Silver
- D: Opals

40

Which son of former Western Australian premier Sir Charles Court became Liberal premier of the same state in 1993?

- A: Victor
- B: Barry
- C: Kenneth
- D: Richard

If you would like to use your 50:50 please turn to page 247
Turn to the answer section on page 258 to find out if you've won $4,000!

7 ◆ $4,000

41

Which of these birds is native to Africa?

A: Ostrich
B: Kiwi
C: Emu
D: Cassowary

42

In the abbreviation PVC, what does the letter C stand for?

A: Cloth
B: Chloride
C: Carbon
D: Cheese

43

Which Australian singer was born Helen Porter Mitchell?

A: Marjorie Lawrence
B: Nellie Melba
C: Gladys Moncrieff
D: Joan Sutherland

44

Which former Beatle narrated the TV adventures of Thomas the Tank Engine?

A: Paul McCartney
B: John Lennon
C: Ringo Starr
D: George Harrison

45

Of aboriginal origin, what is the term for an arm of a river cut off when the water level falls?

A: Arroyo
B: Anabranch
C: Bombora
D: Billabong

If you would like to use your 50:50 please turn to page 247
Turn to the answer section on page 258 to find out if you've won $4,000!

46

Gordon Sumner is the real name of which pop star?

- A: Meat Loaf
- B: Seal
- C: Sting
- D: Boy George

47

Who starred as Fanny Brice in the film musical 'Funny Girl'?

- A: Julie Andrews
- B: Twiggy
- C: Audrey Hepburn
- D: Barbra Streisand

48

Which part of the body would be affected by 'astigmatism'?

- A: Heart
- B: Eyes
- C: Lungs
- D: Hips

49

What essential piece of travelling equipment is a swagman's bluey?

- A: Blanket
- B: Cooking pot
- C: Walking stick
- D: Hat with corks

50

What name is given to the tracks on which tanks and bulldozers run?

- A: Caterpillar
- B: Centipede
- C: Inchworm
- D: Snail

If you would like to use your 50:50 please turn to page 247
Turn to the answer section on page 258 to find out if you've won $4,000!

51

If you ordered 'grenouilles' in a French restaurant, what would you be served?

A: Bread
B: Frogs' legs
C: Wine
D: Onions

52

The Adelaide AFL team has what nickname?

A: Crows
B: Eagles
C: Hawks
D: Magpies

53

Which indigenous Australian was the first person to carry the Sydney Olympic Torch on Australian soil?

A: Nicola Severino
B: Nova Peris-Kneebone
C: Evonne Goolagong-Cawley
D: Ernie Dingo

54

Which writer is best remembered for the classic vampire story 'Dracula'?

A: Mary Shelley
B: Bram Stoker
C: Charles Dickens
D: Jules Verne

55

The Frenchman Andre Ampere gave his name to a unit of what?

A: Time
B: Electrical current
C: Weight
D: Length

If you would like to use your 50:50 please turn to page 247
Turn to the answer section on page 258 to find out if you've won $4,000!

56

In which decade did the Great Train Robbery occur?

A: 1950s
B: 1960s
C: 1970s
D: 1980s

57

The clarinet belongs to which section of the orchestra?

A: String
B: Percussion
C: Brass
D: Woodwind

58

Which country and western singer is famously known as 'The Man in Black'?

A: Kenny Rogers
B: Glenn Campbell
C: Johnny Cash
D: Willie Nelson

59

The American invasion of the Bay of Pigs was an attempt to overthrow the government of which country?

A: Argentina
B: Libya
C: Cuba
D: Iraq

60

On which date did Australia become a federated nation?

A: 1st January, 1900
B: 26th January, 1900
C: 1st January, 1901
D: 26th January, 1901

If you would like to use your 50:50 please turn to page 247
Turn to the answer section on page 258 to find out if you've won $4,000!

61

In what opal town do many of the locals live underground to escape the heat?

A: Oodnadatta
B: Lightning Ridge
C: White Cliffs
D: Coober Pedy

62

Who composed the 'Moonlight Sonata'?

A: Debussy
B: Chopin
C: Dvorak
D: Beethoven

63

Which car emblem consists of four linked circles?

A: Subaru
B: Toyota
C: Citroen
D: Audi

64

What nationality is the operatic tenor Placido Domingo?

A: Italian
B: Mexican
C: Argentinian
D: Spanish

65

What is the nickname of the Australian men's hockey team?

A: Galahs
B: Brolgas
C: Cockatoos
D: Kookaburras

If you would like to use your 50:50 please turn to page 247
Turn to the answer section on page 258 to find out if you've won $4,000!

66

What is mainland Australia's northernmost point?

A: Cape Byron
B: Cape York
C: Steep Point
D: Wilson's Promontory

67

Indian clarified butter used for frying and baking is known as what?

A: Ghee
B: Samosa
C: Korma
D: Biriani

68

Which highway links the Australian state capitals of Brisbane and Sydney?

A: Eyre
B: Bruce
C: Pacific
D: Sturt

69

What symbol is incorporated in the upper left corner of all the Australian state flags?

A: Federation Star
B: Kangaroo
C: Southern Cross
D: Union Jack

70

Artist Tom Roberts was a leader of the what School of Australian painting?

A: Hermannsburg
B: Bundaberg
C: Coburg
D: Heidelberg

If you would like to use your 50:50 please turn to page 247
Turn to the answer section on page 258 to find out if you've won $4,000!

15		$1 MILLION
14		$500,000
13		$250,000
12		$125,000
11		$64,000
10		$32,000
9		$16,000
8	◆	$8,000
7	◆	$4,000
6	◆	$2,000
5	◆	$1,000
4	◆	$500
3	◆	$300
2	◆	$200
1	◆	$100

8 ◆ $8,000

1

What is the correct term for the rotating part of a windmill?

- A: Sails
- B: Propellers
- C: Spinners
- D: Wings

2

What is the name for a short pithy saying such as 'In for a penny, in for a pound'?

- A: Simile
- B: Epithet
- C: Proverb
- D: Analogy

3

Which emperor built a famous wall to limit incursions of Northern tribes into Roman England?

- A: Hadrian
- B: Julius Caesar
- C: Nero
- D: Claudius

4

In which country did the Impressionist art movement begin?

- A: Great Britain
- B: Italy
- C: France
- D: The Netherlands

5

Who assassinated Senator Robert Kennedy in 1968?

- A: Sirhan Sirhan
- B: Lee Harvey Oswald
- C: James Earl Ray
- D: John Wilkes Booth

If you would like to use your 50:50 please turn to page 248
Turn to the answer section on page 259 to find out if you've won $8,000!

6

What is the name for a word made up from initials, such as 'radar' or 'scuba'?

- A: Antonym
- B: Anagram
- C: Acrostic
- D: Acronym

7

What is the chemical symbol for lead?

- A: K
- B: Hg
- C: L
- D: Pb

8

Jacob's Creek is a famous wine-growing location in which valley?

- A: Hunter
- B: Barossa
- C: Clare
- D: Yarra

9

What is the cube of the number eight?

- A: 512
- B: 64
- C: 216
- D: 16

10

Which classic television series starred Jeremy Irons and Anthony Andrews?

- A: Jewel In The Crown
- B: The Far Pavilions
- C: Brideshead Revisited
- D: The Forsyte Saga

If you would like to use your 50:50 please turn to page 248
Turn to the answer section on page 259 to find out if you've won $8,000!

11

What nationality is the Formula One racing driver Mika Hakkinen?

A: Norwegian
B: Swedish
C: Danish
D: Finnish

12

Subject of a criminal libel action was Frank Hardy's 1950 novel 'Power Without what'?

A: Authority
B: Glory
C: Happiness
D: Honour

13

Of which country was Nicolae Ceausescu the president?

A: Bulgaria
B: Romania
C: Hungary
D: East Germany

14

Don Dunstan was the Labor premier of which Australian state throughout the 1970s?

A: South Australia
B: Tasmania
C: Victoria
D: Western Australia

15

Used in dentistry, an amalgam is an alloy of which metal with other metals?

A: Gold
B: Mercury
C: Iron
D: Copper

If you would like to use your 50:50 please turn to page 248
Turn to the answer section on page 259 to find out if you've won $8,000!

8 ◆ $8,000

16

What was the occupation of the man commemorated by Scots on Burns Night?

- A: Soldier
- B: Explorer
- C: Poet
- D: Clan chieftain

17

Which country is nearest to the island of Jersey?

- A: England
- B: Ireland
- C: Spain
- D: France

18

In the 1983 film 'The Big Chill', who played the corpse in the opening credits sequence?

- A: Kevin Costner
- B: Mel Gibson
- C: Tom Hanks
- D: Richard Gere

19

What did the Scottish inventor James Watt help to develop?

- A: Steam engine
- B: Spinning wheel
- C: Radio
- D: Motor car

20

A 'bibliophile' is someone who enjoys which activity?

- A: Drinking
- B: Travelling
- C: Eating
- D: Reading

If you would like to use your 50:50 please turn to page 248
Turn to the answer section on page 259 to find out if you've won $8,000!

21

William Farrer was a pioneer in the development of which industry?

- A: Wool
- B: Wheat
- C: Rice
- D: Iron and steel

22

Which American state saw the first major gold rush in 1848?

- A: Florida
- B: Texas
- C: California
- D: Delaware

23

Thomas Sopwith was famous for designing which type of vehicle?

- A: Aeroplane
- B: Hovercraft
- C: Motorcycle
- D: Train

24

The first Australian to win the Wimbledon men's singles title was Norman who?

- A: Quist
- B: Cooper
- C: Brookes
- D: Hopman

25

Co-founder of the Australian National Naturopathic Association and founder of laboratories producing vitamin, mineral and herbal products was Maurice who?

- A: Kenny
- B: Faulding
- C: Blackmore
- D: Cilento

If you would like to use your 50:50 please turn to page 248
Turn to the answer section on page 259 to find out if you've won $8,000!

26

Who was the British prime minister at the outbreak of World War II?

- A: Winston Churchill
- B: Stanley Baldwin
- C: Neville Chamberlain
- D: Clement Attlee

27

Who became the first woman for over forty years to direct a feature film in Australia when she made 'My Brilliant Career' in 1979?

- A: Gillian Armstrong
- B: Nadia Tass
- C: Jane Campion
- D: Robyn Nevin

28

A novel by Graham Greene, made into a film starring Ralph Fiennes, is titled 'The End of the what'?

- A: Rope
- B: Day
- C: Road
- D: Affair

29

Which group was the subject of the film 'The Great Rock 'N' Roll Swindle'?

- A: The Clash
- B: The Sex Pistols
- C: The Doors
- D: The Who

30

On which currency note does a portrait of the first Australian female member of parliament Edith Cowan appear?

- A: $10
- B: $20
- C: $50
- D: $100

If you would like to use your 50:50 please turn to page 248
Turn to the answer section on page 259 to find out if you've won $8,000!

31

Who composed 'Rhapsody in Blue'?

- A: Cole Porter
- B: Irving Berlin
- C: George Gershwin
- D: Aaron Copland

32

Which fruit comes from bramble bushes?

- A: Strawberry
- B: Blackberry
- C: Gooseberry
- D: Cherry

33

On which river does the city of Vienna stand?

- A: Danube
- B: Rhone
- C: Rhine
- D: Weser

34

The first Australian woman to win an Olympic gold medal was Fanny who?

- A: Durack
- B: Finn
- C: Lightfoot
- D: Gould

35

Which French expression denotes a set meal at a fixed price?

- A: A la carte
- B: Table d'hote
- C: Carte blanche
- D: Cordon bleu

If you would like to use your 50:50 please turn to page 248
Turn to the answer section on page 259 to find out if you've won $8,000!

36

Which currency would you require in the Netherlands?

A: Guilders
B: Marks
C: Schillings
D: Francs

37

Made into a film in 1986 starring Leo McKern and Graham Kennedy, was David Williamson's play 'Travelling where'?

A: North
B: South
C: East
D: West

38

What kind of Italian food is 'ciabatta'?

A: Ham
B: Cheese
C: Ice cream
D: Bread

39

The alimentary canal is primarily involved with which bodily function?

A: Digestion
B: Sight
C: Reproduction
D: Smell

40

What is the name of the peninsula occupied by Spain and Portugal?

A: Balearic Peninsula
B: Hispanic Peninsula
C: Lisboa Peninsula
D: Iberian Peninsula

If you would like to use your 50:50 please turn to page 248
Turn to the answer section on page 259 to find out if you've won $8,000!

41

What name is given to the Japanese art of swordsmanship practised with bamboo staves?

- A: Ju-jitsu
- B: Aikido
- C: Karate
- D: Kendo

42

Which name is given to a pink and white Australian cockatoo?

- A: Captain Cook
- B: Colonel Collins
- C: General George
- D: Major Mitchell

43

Which of these oceans does not lap Australian shores?

- A: Atlantic
- B: Indian
- C: Pacific
- D: Southern

44

Which country produces Mateus Rose wine?

- A: France
- B: Italy
- C: Spain
- D: Portugal

45

Which of these Australian mammals is capable of true flight?

- A: Sugar glider
- B: Wombat
- C: Numbat
- D: Fruit bat

If you would like to use your 50:50 please turn to page 248
Turn to the answer section on page 259 to find out if you've won $8,000!

8 ◆ $8,000

46

To which political party did Prime Minister Ben Chifley belong?

- A: Labor
- B: Liberal
- C: Country
- D: United Australia Party

47

Which saint was especially renowned for his love of nature and reverence for animals?

- A: Francis of Assisi
- B: Nicholas
- C: Anthony
- D: Christopher

48

Staghorns and elkhorns form a genus of which plant?

- A: Fern
- B: Orchid
- C: Cactus
- D: Wattle

49

What is Singapore's basic currency unit?

- A: Dollar
- B: Yen
- C: Dong
- D: Schilling

50

In geography, a tableland is also known by what other term?

- A: Plateau
- B: Continental shelf
- C: Rift valley
- D: Cordillera

If you would like to use your 50:50 please turn to page 248
Turn to the answer section on page 259 to find out if you've won $8,000!

8 ◆ $8,000

51

In 1921, Mao Zedong was a founding member of which Chinese political party?

A: Socialist
B: Kuomintang
C: Communist
D: Nationalist

52

In 1605, who was the leader of the Gunpowder plot to blow up the Houses of Parliament?

A: Colonel Blood
B: Richard Crookback
C: Guy Fawkes
D: Albert Moriarty

53

Which plant is a national emblem of Scotland?

A: Scottish heather
B: Scots pine
C: Scottish primrose
D: Scotch thistle

54

Two essential ingredients of Anzac biscuits are golden syrup and what else?

A: Raisins
B: Rolled oats
C: Citrus peel
D: Peanuts

55

A mark formerly used on convict clothing and other government stores was the broad what?

A: Diamond
B: Axe
C: Arrow
D: Band

If you would like to use your 50:50 please turn to page 248
Turn to the answer section on page 259 to find out if you've won $8,000!

8 ◆ $8,000

56

Emu eggs are a dark shade of which colour?

A: Red
B: Yellow
C: Grey
D: Green

57

An extinct volcano in the extreme south-east of South Australia is Mount what?

A: Gambier
B: Morgan
C: Mulligan
D: Victoria

58

Which order of monks is noted for taking vows of silence?

A: Trappist
B: Franciscan
C: Dominican
D: Capuchin

59

Which famous naturalist visited Australia on the 'Beagle' in 1836?

A: Butler
B: Darwin
C: Wallace
D: Gould

60

Australian Sir Douglas Mawson is famous for his explorations of which continent?

A: Africa
B: Antarctica
C: Asia
D: Australia

If you would like to use your 50:50 please turn to page 248
Turn to the answer section on page 259 to find out if you've won $8,000!

8 ◆ $8,000

61

The liqueur cassis is made from which fruit?

A: Cherry
B: Orange
C: Strawberry
D: Blackcurrant

62

The site of a disused gaol, Fannie Bay is a suburb of which northern Australian city?

A: Townsville
B: Darwin
C: Brisbane
D: Cairns

63

Which VC winner was governor of New South Wales from 1966–81?

A: Hercules Robinson
B: Roden Cutler
C: Mostyn Hanger
D: Day Bosanquet

64

'The Scream' is a famous work by which artist?

A: Edvard Munch
B: Salvador Dali
C: Pablo Picasso
D: Edgar Degas

65

Australian George Johnston wrote the 1964 novel 'My Brother who'?

A: Jack
B: James
C: Jeff
D: John

If you would like to use your 50:50 please turn to page 248
Turn to the answer section on page 259 to find out if you've won $8,000!

66

Australian John Williams is a maestro of which musical instrument?

A: Piano

B: Guitar

C: Cello

D: Violin

If you would like to use your 50:50 please turn to page 248
Turn to the answer section on page 259 to find out if you've won $8,000!

50:50

15		$1 MILLION
14		$500,000
13		$250,000
12		$125,000
11		$64,000
10		$32,000
9	◆	$16,000
8	◆	$8,000
7	◆	$4,000
6	◆	$2,000
5	◆	$1,000
4	◆	$500
3	◆	$300
2	◆	$200
1	◆	$100

9 ◆ $16,000

1

In darts, how many points is the outer bull's-eye worth?

A: 20
B: 25
C: 40
D: 50

2

Who played Nicole Kidman's husband in the 1995 movie 'To Die For'?

A: Matt Dillon
B: Tom Cruise
C: Rob Lowe
D: Brad Pitt

3

Which garment is secured by a sash called an 'obi'?

A: Kimono
B: Sari
C: Jellaba
D: Judo robe

4

Mt. Wellington overlooks which Australian state capital city?

A: Melbourne
B: Adelaide
C: Hobart
D: Brisbane

5

Which fictional resort is terrorised by a great white shark in the film 'Jaws'?

A: Long Beach
B: Bodega Bay
C: Newport News
D: Amity Island

If you would like to use your 50:50 please turn to page 249
Turn to the answer section on page 259 to find out if you've won $16,000!

9 ◆ $16,000

6

Which Hollywood star made an early appearance in the 1984 film 'BMX Bandits'?

A: Michelle Pfeiffer
B: Julia Roberts
C: Nicole Kidman
D: Meg Ryan

7

What was the full first name of gangster Al Capone?

A: Alan
B: Alfredo
C: Alphonse
D: Alberto

8

What is lithium?

A: A metal
B: A gas
C: A fossil
D: A rock

9

Where is the Yukon river?

A: Europe
B: Asia
C: Africa
D: North America

10

In which country is the opera Aida set?

A: India
B: Egypt
C: China
D: Thailand

If you would like to use your 50:50 please turn to page 249
Turn to the answer section on page 259 to find out if you've won $16,000!

11

Which battles took place between the Royal Houses of York and Lancaster?

- A: Thirty Years War
- B: Hundred Years War
- C: Wars Of The Roses
- D: English Civil War

12

The southern headland of what bay located on the New South Wales coast is actually part of the ACT?

- A: Jervis
- B: Batemans
- C: Twofold
- D: Disaster

13

Art critic and writer Robert Hughes' 1987 book on early Australia is titled 'The Fatal what'?

- A: Shore
- B: Journey
- C: Start
- D: Destiny

14

Which Federal Labor attorney-general was the main architect of the bill for the Family Law Act introduced in Parliament in 1975?

- A: Jim Cairns
- B: Bill Hayden
- C: Lionel Murphy
- D: Frank Crean

15

Who directed the 1992 film 'The Crying Game'?

- A: Alan Parker
- B: Neil Jordan
- C: Steven Spielberg
- D: Stephen Frears

If you would like to use your 50:50 please turn to page 249
Turn to the answer section on page 259 to find out if you've won $16,000!

16

In which religion is the Aga Khan a leader?

- A: Buddhism
- B: Islam
- C: Hinduism
- D: Christianity

17

In which city was Wolfgang Amadeus Mozart born?

- A: Salzburg
- B: Vienna
- C: Berlin
- D: Prague

18

What Australian living thing is a kurrajong?

- A: Bird
- B: Fish
- C: Flower
- D: Tree

19

At which Australian town did Japanese prisoners of war attempt a mass break out in 1944?

- A: Corowa
- B: Cowra
- C: Noosa
- D: Nowra

20

Of which Australian state was Sir Henry Bolte premier from 1955 to 1972?

- A: New South Wales
- B: Tasmania
- C: Queensland
- D: Victoria

If you would like to use your 50:50 please turn to page 249
Turn to the answer section on page 259 to find out if you've won $16,000!

21

What kind of show did Charles Cruft establish in Britain in the 19th century?

- A: Dog show
- B: Boat show
- C: Circus
- D: Quiz show

22

In which year of World War II did the Battle of the Coral Sea take place?

- A: 1939
- B: 1940
- C: 1942
- D: 1945

23

Which of these is a Sikh place of worship?

- A: Mosque
- B: Cathedral
- C: Synagogue
- D: Gurdwara

24

What is the collective term for a group of kangaroos?

- A: Gang
- B: Mob
- C: Posse
- D: Pride

25

Which word on champagne or sparkling wine labels indicates that it is dry?

- A: Sec
- B: Brut
- C: Premier Cru
- D: Doux

If you would like to use your 50:50 please turn to page 249
Turn to the answer section on page 259 to find out if you've won $16,000!

26

Which of these is not a name for the star of Ken Hall's 1934 comedy film 'Strike Me Lucky'?

- A: Mo
- B: Roy Rene
- C: Harry van der Sluys
- D: George Wallace

27

Who composed the music for the ballet 'Swan Lake'?

- A: Chopin
- B: Tchaikovsky
- C: Liszt
- D: Stravinsky

28

Named after its chairman was which 1987-89 Queensland inquiry into 'possible illegal activities and associated police misconduct'?

- A: Muirhead
- B: Costigan
- C: Fitzgerald
- D: Woodward

29

Which Shakespeare play begins with the words, 'If music be the food of love, play on . . . '?

- A: Twelfth Night
- B: Antony and Cleopatra
- C: All's Well That Ends Well
- D: Romeo and Juliet

30

Who discovered X-rays?

- A: Thomas Edison
- B: John Logie Baird
- C: Marie Curie
- D: Wilhelm Roentgen

If you would like to use your 50:50 please turn to page 249
Turn to the answer section on page 259 to find out if you've won $16,000!

9 ◆ $16,000

31

What is the most famous tourist attraction in Lake Havasu City, Arizona?

- A: London Bridge
- B: The Grand Canyon
- C: Niagara Falls
- D: Abraham Lincoln's birthplace

32

In academia, a B.Litt. is literally a Bachelor of what?

- A: Literacy
- B: Lithology
- C: Lithography
- D: Letters

33

What was introduced in January 1917, but abandoned the same year due to public pressure?

- A: Daylight saving
- B: Conscription
- C: Early hotel closing
- D: ID cards

34

Which pop group took its name from a character in the science fiction film 'Barbarella'?

- A: Depeche Mode
- B: Def Leppard
- C: Duran Duran
- D: Deep Purple

35

Three score years and ten add up to what number?

- A: 60
- B: 70
- C: 80
- D: 90

If you would like to use your 50:50 please turn to page 249
Turn to the answer section on page 259 to find out if you've won $16,000!

36

Yachtsmen from which nation won the America's Cup in 1995?

- A: Italy
- B: Australia
- C: USA
- D: New Zealand

37

The Sydney 2000 Olympics were formally known as the Games of the 'what' Olympiad?

- A: 24th
- B: 25th
- C: 26th
- D: 27th

38

By what name is the mature female of the red kangaroo known?

- A: Blue flyer
- B: Blue heeler
- C: Eastern grey
- D: Grey flyer

39

The Razorbacks are a Sydney-based team in which sport?

- A: Baseball
- B: Basketball
- C: Rugby League
- D: Soccer

40

The Japanese call their country Nippon or Nihon, meaning source of the what?

- A: Moon
- B: Sun
- C: Tides
- D: Winds

If you would like to use your 50:50 please turn to page 249
Turn to the answer section on page 259 to find out if you've won $16,000!

9 ◆ $16,000

41

To which religion do the majority of the people of India belong?

- A: Hindu
- B: Parsee
- C: Buddhist
- D: Shinto

42

Which anniversary of the start of the Korean War was commemorated in June, 2000?

- A: 50th
- B: 60th
- C: 70th
- D: 80th

43

On which Indonesian island is the city of Jakarta?

- A: Sumatra
- B: Java
- C: Sulawesi
- D: Bali

44

The sad story of the Japanese beauty Cho-Cho-san is told in which opera by Puccini?

- A: Tosca
- B: Turandot
- C: The Mikado
- D: Madame Butterfly

45

In area, which is the largest country in South America?

- A: Argentina
- B: Chile
- C: Brazil
- D: Bolivia

If you would like to use your 50:50 please turn to page 249
Turn to the answer section on page 259 to find out if you've won $16,000!

46

What number is represented by 'MCM' in Roman numerals?

A: 900
B: 1400
C: 1900
D: 2900

47

As leader of the New South Wales Builders' Labourers Federation, Jack Mundey was famous for inaugurating bans of what colour?

A: Black
B: Blue
C: Green
D: Pink

48

Militant trade unionist Norm Gallagher was employed in which industry?

A: Building construction
B: Banking
C: Metal workers
D: Waterside workers

49

Which Oscar for 1994 was won by Australians Lizzie Gardiner and Tim Chappel?

A: Original Screenplay
B: Visual Effects
C: Costume Design
D: Original Song

50

Mountains and desert make up two thirds of the three and a half million square miles of which country?

A: Japan
B: Bangladesh
C: Nepal
D: China

If you would like to use your 50:50 please turn to page 249
Turn to the answer section on page 259 to find out if you've won $16,000!

9 ◆ $16,000

51

Which of the following did not star in television's hugely successful 'The Mavis Brampton Show'?

- A: Garry McDonald
- B: Barry Creyton
- C: Gordon Chater
- D: Carole Raye

52

In 1795, Bass and Flinders explored the coastline south of Botany Bay in a small boat of what name?

- A: Jolly Roger
- B: Tom Thumb
- C: Thumbelina
- D: Digit Dick

53

Sofia is the capital of which country?

- A: Algeria
- B: Argentina
- C: Bulgaria
- D: Portugal

54

At around 480 km, the world's longest straight stretch of railway is located between the towns of Watson, South Australia and Nurina, where?

- A: Northern Territory
- B: Queensland
- C: Victoria
- D: Western Australia

55

Which Gilbert and Sullivan operetta has the alternative title 'The Lass That Loved A Sailor'?

- A: Ruddigore
- B: The Pirates of Penzance
- C: HMS Pinafore
- D: The Gondoliers

If you would like to use your 50:50 please turn to page 249
Turn to the answer section on page 259 to find out if you've won $16,000!

56

With black and yellow markings thought to resemble Aboriginal body-painting, which amphibian has the kind named corroboree?

- A: Salamander
- B: Newt
- C: Frog
- D: Toad

57

Which Australian boxing champion died tragically young from an illness in the USA in 1917?

- A: Vic Patrick
- B: Colin Bell
- C: Dave Sands
- D: Les Darcy

58

In 2002, Queen Elizabeth II celebrates which number anniversary on the throne?

- A: 30th
- B: 40th
- C: 50th
- D: 60th

59

A pre-arranged parliamentary question asked specifically to allow a propagandist reply by a minister is a Dorothy who?

- A: Dix
- B: Gale
- C: Dandridge
- D: Lamour

60

What high office did Alfred Deakin first assume in 1903?

- A: Attorney-General
- B: Treasurer
- C: Chief Justice
- D: Prime Minister

If you would like to use your 50:50 please turn to page 249
Turn to the answer section on page 259 to find out if you've won $16,000!

9 ◆ $16,000

61

What is Queensland's state floral emblem?

- A: Kangaroo paw
- B: Common heath
- C: Cooktown orchid
- D: Sturt's desert pea

62

In which position on the field does soccer star Mark Bosnich usually play for Australia?

- A: Goalkeeper
- B: Midfielder
- C: Striker
- D: Sweeper

If you would like to use your 50:50 please turn to page 249
Turn to the answer section on page 259 to find out if you've won $16,000!

15 $1 MILLION
14 $500,000
13 $250,000
12 $125,000
11 $64,000
10 ◆ $32,000
9 ◆ $16,000
8 ◆ $8,000
7 ◆ $4,000
6 ◆ $2,000
5 ◆ $1,000
4 ◆ $500
3 ◆ $300
2 ◆ $200
1 ◆ $100

1

Who co-wrote the song 'Do They Know It's Christmas' with Bob Geldof?

A: David Bowie
B: Midge Ure
C: Phil Collins
D: Paul McCartney

2

Which sea laps the east coast of Scotland?

A: North
B: Caspian
C: Baltic
D: Irish

3

Which city replaced Calcutta as India's capital in 1912?

A: Delhi
B: Bombay
C: Colombo
D: Madras

4

Who invented the spinning jenny?

A: Richard Arkwright
B: James Hargreaves
C: James Watt
D: Samuel Crompton

5

A banshee is a spirit in the folklore of which people?

A: Basque
B: Irish
C: American Indian
D: Maori

If you would like to use your 50:50 please turn to page 250
Turn to the answer section on page 260 to find out if you've won $32,000!

6

Which religious movement was founded by Mary Baker Eddy?

- A: Jehovah's Witnesses
- B: Christian Science
- C: Salvation Army
- D: 7th-Day Adventists

7

Which king was killed at the Battle of Hastings?

- A: William
- B: John
- C: Edward
- D: Harold

8

Which seat did Pauline Hanson win as an Independent in the 1996 federal election?

- A: Bennelong
- B: Dickson
- C: Oxley
- D: Wills

9

What was the name of the world's first test-tube baby?

- A: Louise Brown
- B: Sarah Evans
- C: Lucy Bryant
- D: Sharon Fuller

10

In what artistic occupation is Australian Richard Bonynge internationally renowned?

- A: Conductor
- B: Ballet dancer
- C: Actor
- D: Violinist

If you would like to use your 50:50 please turn to page 250
Turn to the answer section on page 260 to find out if you've won $32,000!

11

By what name is the baobab tree better known in Australia?

- A: Bottle tree
- B: Banyan
- C: Banyalla
- D: Bangalow

12

Which of these great Australian opera singers is known by her original name?

- A: Florence Austral
- B: June Bronhill
- C: Nellie Melba
- D: Joan Sutherland

13

In which city is the Hermitage Museum?

- A: Paris
- B: Helsinki
- C: Copenhagen
- D: Saint Petersburg

14

Which character in the Sherlock Holmes stories was an Inspector from Scotland Yard?

- A: Lestrade
- B: Hudson
- C: Mycroft
- D: Watson

15

How many times was Australia's Jack Brabham the world Formula One drivers' champion?

- A: Once
- B: Two
- C: Three
- D: Four

If you would like to use your 50:50 please turn to page 250
Turn to the answer section on page 260 to find out if you've won $32,000!

16

Which of these island groups is situated in the Indian Ocean?

A: Canary Islands | B: Hawaii
C: Bahamas | D: Maldives

17

The late Sir Mark Oliphant specialised in which field of science?

A: Astronomy | B: Biochemistry
C: Medicine | D: Physics

18

What nationality is former World Motor Racing Champion Keke Rosberg?

A: Belgian | B: Swedish
C: Danish | D: Finnish

19

In which country is Fez, home of the famous hat?

A: Turkey | B: Morocco
C: Algeria | D: Tunisia

20

Which is the largest city in the USA's largest state?

A: Dallas | B: Los Angeles
C: New York | D: Anchorage

If you would like to use your 50:50 please turn to page 250
Turn to the answer section on page 260 to find out if you've won $32,000!

10 ◆ $32,000

21

In which year did an earthquake cause extensive damage to the New South Wales city of Newcastle?

- A: 1987
- B: 1988
- C: 1989
- D: 1990

22

Which of these spices comes from tree bark?

- A: Turmeric
- B: Cinnamon
- C: Nutmeg
- D: Ginger

23

By what name is Camille Javal better known?

- A: Brigitte Bardot
- B: Greta Garbo
- C: Marlene Dietrich
- D: Jeanne Moreau

24

What is the sum of the interior angles of a triangle?

- A: 360 degrees
- B: 90 degrees
- C: 180 degrees
- D: 3 degrees

25

Who wrote 'Das Kapital'?

- A: Lenin
- B: Stalin
- C: Trotsky
- D: Marx

If you would like to use your 50:50 please turn to page 250
Turn to the answer section on page 260 to find out if you've won $32,000!

26

Where did Moses receive the Ten Commandments?

- A: Mount Ararat
- B: Mount of Olives
- C: Mount Sinai
- D: Mount Olympus

27

Who was the third president of the United States?

- A: Thomas Jefferson
- B: John Adams
- C: Abraham Lincoln
- D: James Madison

28

Who wrote the opera 'Turandot'?

- A: Verdi
- B: Rossini
- C: Bellini
- D: Puccini

29

What is a positive electrode called?

- A: Anode
- B: Cathode
- C: Diode
- D: Triode

30

In boxing, which of these categories is closest in weight to flyweight?

- A: Featherweight
- B: Bantamweight
- C: Lightweight
- D: Welterweight

If you would like to use your 50:50 please turn to page 250
Turn to the answer section on page 260 to find out if you've won $32,000!

31

What was Peter Cosgrove's rank as leader of the InterFET forces in East Timor?

- A: General
- B: Brigadier general
- C: Lieutenant general
- D: Major general

32

A colour variant of the greengrocer, a black prince is which insect?

- A: Grasshopper
- B: Slater
- C: Cicada
- D: Cricket

33

What does 'impecunious' mean?

- A: Poor
- B: Cheeky
- C: Bald
- D: Ugly

34

Which natural disaster occurred at Meckering, WA, in October, 1968?

- A: Flood
- B: Tornado
- C: Earthquake
- D: Bushfire

35

Film director, Dr. George Miller is a graduate in which profession?

- A: Law
- B: Veterinary science
- C: Medicine
- D: Engineering

If you would like to use your 50:50 please turn to page 250
Turn to the answer section on page 260 to find out if you've won $32,000!

36

What instrument does a 'timpanist' play?

A: Snare drum
B: Steel drum
C: Bass drum
D: Kettle drum

37

The Blake Prize is awarded annually in which special subject area of painting, drawing or sculpture?

A: Religious art
B: Landscape
C: Portraiture
D: Genre

38

For most of its length, the International Date Line is how many degrees away from the Prime Meridian?

A: 90 degrees
B: 100 degrees
C: 180 degrees
D: 360 degrees

39

Who led a slaves' revolt against Rome in 73 BC?

A: Spartacus
B: Mark Antony
C: Brutus
D: Ben Hur

40

'Poppy' and 'After Venice' are works by which dancer and choreographer?

A: Robert Helpmann
B: Graeme Murphy
C: Twyla Tharp
D: Maina Gielgud

If you would like to use your 50:50 please turn to page 250
Turn to the answer section on page 260 to find out if you've won $32,000!

10 ◆ $32,000

41

Which painter had the surname Van Rijn?

A: Michelangelo
B: Rembrandt
C: Magritte
D: Titian

42

Which of these religions was founded first?

A: Buddhism
B: Christianity
C: Islam
D: Sikhism

43

Before undertaking his ill-fated expedition in 1860, Robert O'Hara Burke was employed in which area of public administration?

A: Prisons
B: Police
C: Schools
D: Hospitals

44

What is the literal meaning of the word 'gymnasium'?

A: Exercise hall
B: Physical fitness
C: Exercise naked
D: Keeping fit

45

In 1894, which Australian state was the first colony to give women the right to vote?

A: Queensland
B: New South Wales
C: South Australia
D: Tasmania

If you would like to use your 50:50 please turn to page 250
Turn to the answer section on page 260 to find out if you've won $32,000!

46

The world's largest deposit of which mineral has been mined at Weipa since 1960?

- A: Uranium
- B: Copper
- C: Bauxite
- D: Manganese

47

How many senators represent each state in the federal parliament?

- A: 6
- B: 8
- C: 10
- D: 12

48

Australian stage actress Ruth Cracknell has written a memoir titled 'Journey from where'?

- A: Venice
- B: Florence
- C: Rome
- D: Paris

49

The Anzac forces at Gallipoli were commanded by William who?

- A: Birdwood
- B: Bennett
- C: Birdseye
- D: Birch

50

Which famous Dutch ship was wrecked at Houtman Abrolhos on the west coast of Australia in 1629?

- A: Duyfken
- B: Sardham
- C: Cygnet
- D: Batavia

If you would like to use your 50:50 please turn to page 250
Turn to the answer section on page 260 to find out if you've won $32,000!

10 ◆ $32,000

51

What was the name of the ship of underwater explorer, Jacques Cousteau?

- A: Echo
- B: Calypso
- C: Ariadne
- D: Daphne

52

Common in northern and eastern Australia during summer, the koel or cooeebird is a species of which bird?

- A: Parrot
- B: Cuckoo
- C: Curlew
- D: Wren

53

Which Noel Coward play formed the basis for the classic film 'Brief Encounter'?

- A: Blithe Spirit
- B: The Vortex
- C: Still Life
- D: Private Lives

54

Which singer was known as 'The Swedish Nightingale'?

- A: Adelina Patti
- B: Maria Callas
- C: Jenny Lind
- D: Nellie Melba

55

Which Australian painter and sculptor who died in 1999, bequeathed to the nation his Shoalhaven River property, 'Bundanon'?

- A: John Perceval
- B: John Olsen
- C: Arthur Boyd
- D: Brett Whiteley

If you would like to use your 50:50 please turn to page 250
Turn to the answer section on page 260 to find out if you've won $32,000!

56

Who replaced the ailing Ringo Starr for part of the Beatles' Australian tour in 1964?

- A: Pete Best
- B: Brian Epstein
- C: Stuart Sutcliffe
- D: Jimmy Nicol

57

Having a Norwegian ancestry, which Australian writer's original surname was Larsen?

- A: Henry Lawson
- B: Rolf Boldrewood
- C: Marcus Clarke
- D: Norman Lindsay

58

Twenty-fourth July, 2000, marked the 100th anniversary of the first award to an Australian of which highest military honour?

- A: George Cross
- B: Medal of Honour
- C: Victoria Cross
- D: Medal of Valour

If you would like to use your 50:50 please turn to page 250
Turn to the answer section on page 260 to find out if you've won $32,000!

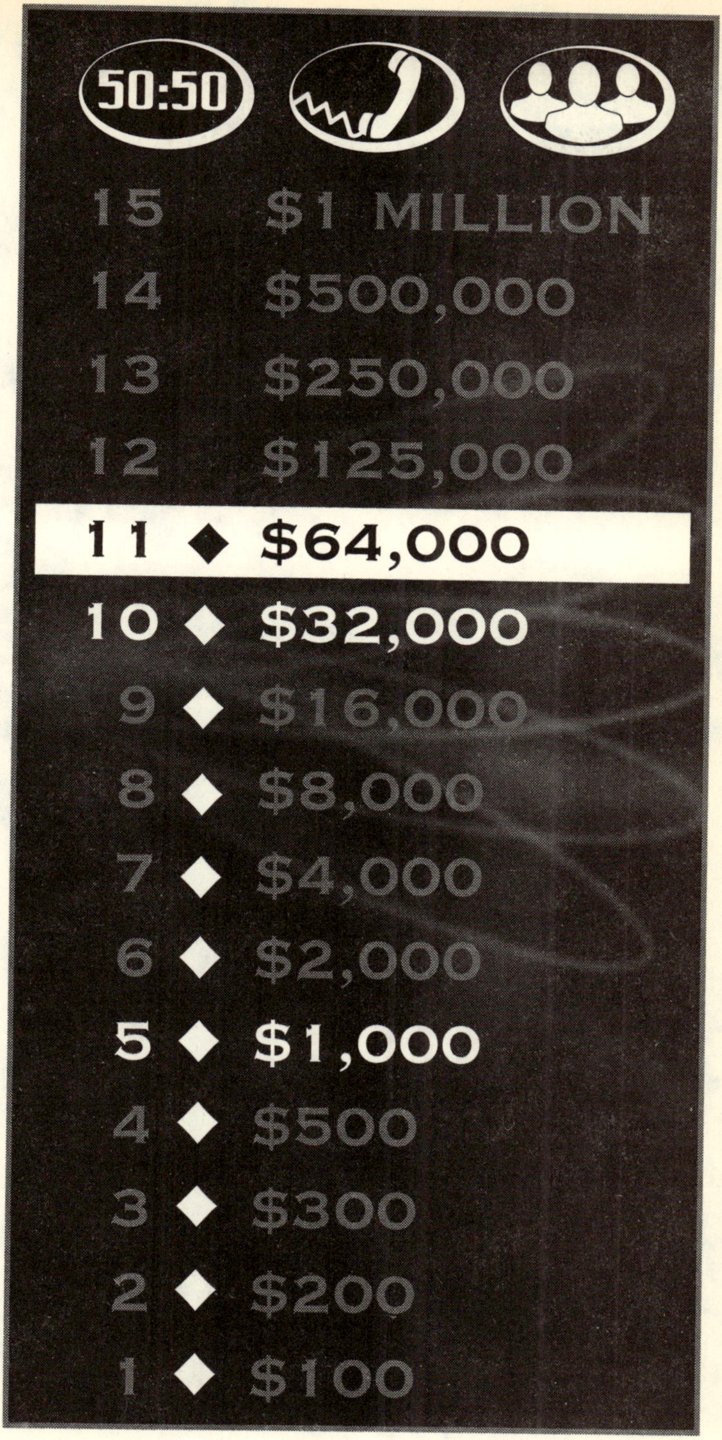
50:50
15 $1 MILLION
14 $500,000
13 $250,000
12 $125,000
11 ◆ $64,000
10 ◆ $32,000
9 ◆ $16,000
8 ◆ $8,000
7 ◆ $4,000
6 ◆ $2,000
5 ◆ $1,000
4 ◆ $500
3 ◆ $300
2 ◆ $200
1 ◆ $100

11 ◆ $64,000

1

The name of which chemical element is derived from the Greek word for 'sun'?

- A: Radon
- B: Helium
- C: Argon
- D: Oxygen

2

Which Queensland city was named after a British Prime Minister?

- A: Gladstone
- B: Bowen
- C: Townsville
- D: Mackay

3

In Egyptian mythology, which of these became ruler of the underworld?

- A: Osiris
- B: Ra
- C: Isis
- D: Horus

4

Which of these dances originated in Poland?

- A: Waltz
- B: Mazurka
- C: Polka
- D: Jive

5

The game mah-jong takes its name from the Chinese word meaning what?

- A: Sparrows
- B: Dragons
- C: Ribbons
- D: Goldfish

If you would like to use your 50:50 please turn to page 251
Turn to the answer section on page 260 to find out if you've won $64,000!

6

Which country is the world's largest producer of coal?

- A: India
- B: Russia
- C: China
- D: USA

7

Which of the following vitamins is also called 'retinol'?

- A: Vitamin A
- B: Vitamin B2
- C: Vitamin E
- D: Vitamin K

8

Niagara Falls, on the border between the USA and Canada, are situated on which river?

- A: Niagara
- B: Erie
- C: Ontario
- D: St Lawrence

9

Boxer Johnny Famechon won a world title in which weight division?

- A: Fly
- B: Bantam
- C: Feather
- D: Light

10

How many stars are on the flag of New Zealand?

- A: Four
- B: Five
- C: Six
- D: Seven

If you would like to use your 50:50 please turn to page 251
Turn to the answer section on page 260 to find out if you've won $64,000!

11 ◆ $64,000

11

Born in 1886, what was the first name of Rupert Murdoch's journalist father?

A: Alan
B: Harvey
C: Keith
D: Roger

12

On which river does Baghdad stand?

A: Tigris
B: Euphrates
C: Jordan
D: Bosporus

13

How are Dominican monks also known?

A: Whitefriars
B: Greyfriars
C: Blackfriars
D: Trappists

14

What does the letter F indicate on a Plimsoll line?

A: Fresh water
B: Full
C: Freight
D: Fuel

15

Captain Cook's ship Endeavour, was formerly a collier with what name?

A: Marquis of Queensberry
B: Earl of Pembroke
C: Whitby
D: Pelican

If you would like to use your 50:50 please turn to page 251
Turn to the answer section on page 260 to find out if you've won $64,000!

16

A fierce hunter, the Australian hobby is otherwise known as the little what?

- A: Owl
- B: Butcher bird
- C: Falcon
- D: Eagle

17

Which of these presidents was not a Republican?

- A: Gerald Ford
- B: Richard Nixon
- C: George Bush
- D: Jimmy Carter

18

Which of these people was alive in the year 100 BC?

- A: Hannibal
- B: Julius Caesar
- C: Confucius
- D: Cleopatra

19

If a chemical substance is 'volatile', what is it likely to form?

- A: Acid
- B: Vapour
- C: Compound
- D: Liquid

20

In terms of population, what is the largest Portuguese speaking city in the world?

- A: Lisbon
- B: Rio de Janeiro
- C: Sao Paulo
- D: Oporto

If you would like to use your 50:50 please turn to page 251
Turn to the answer section on page 260 to find out if you've won $64,000!

21

Before becoming vice president of the USA, Al Gore was a senator for which state?

- A: Alabama
- B: Mississippi
- C: Florida
- D: Tennessee

22

In which body of water is the Isle of Man?

- A: North Sea
- B: Irish Sea
- C: Cardigan Bay
- D: Bristol Channel

23

Directed by Joseph Perry, the 1900 film 'Soldiers of the Cross' was made under the auspices of which organisation?

- A: Red Cross
- B: Salvation Army
- C: Methodist Church
- D: Legacy

24

The new Federal Parliament House was opened in which year?

- A: 1984
- B: 1986
- C: 1987
- D: 1988

25

Which of these primates live on the Rock of Gibraltar?

- A: Orangutans
- B: Chimpanzees
- C: Barbary apes
- D: Baboons

If you would like to use your 50:50 please turn to page 251
Turn to the answer section on page 260 to find out if you've won $64,000!

26

By winning at Wimbledon in 2000, US tennis star Pete Sampras broke which Australian's long-standing record of 12 grand slam men's singles titles?

- A: Roy Emerson
- B: Rod Laver
- C: John Newcombe
- D: Frank Sedgman

27

What was the pen name of the author Eric Blair?

- A: George Eliot
- B: George Bernard Shaw
- C: George Orwell
- D: Georges Simenon

28

Who was the Australian cycling Olympic gold medallist killed in a road accident in 1958?

- A: Lionel Cox
- B: Dunc Gray
- C: Russell Mockridge
- D: Kevin Sefton

29

In which mountain range is K2, the second highest mountain in the world?

- A: Karakoram
- B: Himalayas
- C: Hindu Kush
- D: Urals

30

Which salad vegetable belongs to the same family as the poisonous 'deadly nightshade'?

- A: Tomato
- B: Radish
- C: Cucumber
- D: Beetroot

If you would like to use your 50:50 please turn to page 251
Turn to the answer section on page 260 to find out if you've won $64,000!

31

Grunge music originated in which American city?

A: Seattle
B: Pittsburgh
C: Detroit
D: Boston

32

What sort of creature is Gandalf in JRR Tolkien's novel 'The Hobbit'?

A: Elf
B: Dragon
C: Wizard
D: Goblin

33

Which snake is the only adder native to Australia?

A: Puff adder
B: Night adder
C: Common adder
D: Death adder

34

Which of these Peter Carey novels did not win the Miles Franklin Award?

A: Bliss
B: Illywhacker
C: Jack Maggs
D: Oscar and Lucinda

35

Which Australian film concerns the staging of a Mozart opera?

A: Radiance
B: Proof
C: Praise
D: Cosi

If you would like to use your 50:50 please turn to page 251
Turn to the answer section on page 260 to find out if you've won $64,000!

36

What type of mammal is the Australian quokka?

A: Bandicoot
B: Possum
C: Rodent
D: Wallaby

37

Who wrote the Miles Franklin Award-winning novel 'Cloudstreet'?

A: Thea Astley
B: Kate Grenville
C: Peter Corris
D: Tim Winton

38

Which Australian swimmer won the 200m Freestyle gold medal at the 1988 Seoul Olympics?

A: Duncan Armstrong
B: Jon Sieben
C: Mark Stockwell
D: Rob Woodhouse

39

Which Australian actor is especially remembered for his performances in the one-man play 'The Elocution of Benjamin Franklin'?

A: Gordon Chater
B: John Meillon
C: Barry Creyton
D: Ron Haddrick

40

Because only about 3,000 were struck, the penny of which year is the most famous rare Australian coin?

A: 1920
B: 1930
C: 1940
D: 1950

If you would like to use your 50:50 please turn to page 251
Turn to the answer section on page 260 to find out if you've won $64,000!

41

Which artistic movement was founded by Hunt, Millais and Rossetti?

A: Surrealists
B: Arts and Crafts
C: Fauvists
D: Pre-Raphaelites

42

What was the first bird Noah let out of the Ark?

A: Owl
B: Raven
C: Dove
D: Skylark

43

How many degrees are there in an 'octant'?

A: 45
B: 60
C: 75
D: 90

44

What does a numismatist collect?

A: Stamps
B: Fossils
C: Teddy bears
D: Coins

45

What kind of bridge is the Golden Gate Bridge?

A: Cantilever
B: Bascule
C: Suspension
D: Steel arch

If you would like to use your 50:50 please turn to page 251
Turn to the answer section on page 260 to find out if you've won $64,000!

46

On Father's Day in 1984, seven people were shot dead in Sydney because of a clash between the Bandidos and which other rival bikie gang?

- A: Comanches
- B: Comancheros
- C: Commandos
- D: Conquistadores

If you would like to use your 50:50 please turn to page 251
Turn to the answer section on page 260 to find out if you've won $64,000!

15 $1 MILLION
14 $500,000
13 $250,000
12 ◆ $125,000
11 ◆ $64,000
10 ◆ $32,000
9 ◆ $16,000
8 ◆ $8,000
7 ◆ $4,000
6 ◆ $2,000
5 ◆ $1,000
4 ◆ $500
3 ◆ $300
2 ◆ $200
1 ◆ $100

12 ◆ $125,000

1

What was the first vineyard established in the Barossa Valley?

A: Orlando
B: Penfolds
C: Seppelt
D: Yalumba

2

What is a trumpet manucode?

A: Tropical bird
B: Beetle
C: Musical instrument
D: Hearing device

3

Who wrote the 1915 classic of polar exploration, 'The Home of the Blizzard'?

A: John Davis
B: Ernest Shackleton
C: Douglas Mawson
D: Edgeworth David

4

Which poison is obtained from wolf's-bane?

A: Strychnine
B: Aconite
C: Curare
D: Cyanide

5

Which modern country is the region known in ancient times as Cappadocia?

A: Greece
B: Turkey
C: Bulgaria
D: Romania

If you would like to use your 50:50 please turn to page 252
Turn to the answer section on page 260 to find out if you've won $125,000!

6

What structure has two basic types called 'gravity' and 'arch'?

A: Bridge
B: Dam
C: Pier
D: Road

7

Balls Pyramid is a basalt pinnacle located off the east coast of Australia near which island?

A: Great Sandy
B: Hook
C: Lord Howe
D: Norfolk

8

Which Australian athlete won the 80m Hurdles at the 1968 Mexico City Olympics?

A: Pam Kilborn
B: Marilyn Black
C: Maureen Caird
D: Jennifer Lamy

9

Who was Australia's only Tasmanian-born prime minister of the 20th century?

A: Arthur Fadden
B: Joseph Lyons
C: George Reid
D: James Scullin

10

Which part of an animal's body is known as the 'carapace'?

A: Shell
B: Snout
C: Hoof
D: Tail

If you would like to use your 50:50 please turn to page 252
Turn to the answer section on page 260 to find out if you've won $125,000!

11

What was 'Che' Guevara's real first name?

A: Ernesto
B: Alfredo
C: Edmundo
D: Ricardo

12

Which of these is a former name for the Russian city of Volgograd?

A: Leningrad
B: St Petersburg
C: Minsk
D: Stalingrad

13

In American football, which team won the most Super Bowls in the 1980s?

A: Washington Redskins
B: Chicago Bears
C: New York Giants
D: San Francisco 49ers

14

'Varicella' is the technical term for which disease?

A: Scarlet fever
B: Chickenpox
C: Diabetes
D: Measles

15

What type of living thing is the dugite of south-western Australia?

A: Lizard
B: Marsupial
C: Snake
D: Tree

If you would like to use your 50:50 please turn to page 252
Turn to the answer section on page 260 to find out if you've won $125,000!

16

Who unofficially cut the ribbon at the opening of the Sydney Harbour Bridge in 1932?

- A: Sir Philip Game
- B: Francis De Groot
- C: Sir Isaac Isaacs
- D: Jack Lang

17

Which British comedian committed suicide in Sydney in 1968?

- A: Tony Hancock
- B: Frankie Howerd
- C: Sid James
- D: Kenneth Williams

18

How many Olympic gold medals did champion Australian athlete Ron Clarke win?

- A: None
- B: One
- C: Two
- D: Three

19

The wreckage of what airliner was found in the Snowy Mountains 27 years after it disappeared on a flight in 1931?

- A: Kyeema
- B: Miss Hobart
- C: Southern Cloud
- D: Stella Australis

20

In Australia, what is Geraldton wax?

- A: Plant
- B: Pest
- C: Floor polish
- D: Ear problem

If you would like to use your 50:50 please turn to page 252
Turn to the answer section on page 260 to find out if you've won $125,000!

21

What commercially important fish was formerly known as hake?

A: Flathead
B: Ocean perch
C: Gemfish
D: Ling

22

Balboa made the first recorded European sighting of which ocean in 1513?

A: Atlantic
B: Indian
C: Arctic
D: Pacific

23

The heroic Australian nurse and prisoner-of-war who survived the Banka Island massacre by Japanese soldiers, was Vivian who?

A: Thompson
B: Bullwinkel
C: Shaw
D: Cavell

24

In commemoration of which monarch's birthday did Australians once celebrate Empire Day on the 24th March?

A: George III
B: George IV
C: Edward VII
D: Victoria

25

Written in 1939 while still living in England, what was Patrick White's first novel?

A: The Eye of the Storm
B: Happy Valley
C: The Tree of Man
D: Voss

If you would like to use your 50:50 please turn to page 252
Turn to the answer section on page 260 to find out if you've won $125,000!

12 ◆ $125,000

26

Springfield is the capital of which American state?

A: Illinois
B: Michigan
C: Missouri
D: Ohio

27

In which of the arts was Charles Conder a prominent Australian?

A: Literature
B: Painting
C: Music
D: Sculpture

28

The Dominican Republic is situated on which island?

A: Hispaniola
B: Puerto Rico
C: Cuba
D: Dominica

29

Which Australian prime minister died in office just before the end of World War II?

A: Chifley
B: Scullin
C: Lyons
D: Curtin

30

With which athletics event is Bob Beamon most associated?

A: Triple jump
B: Pole vault
C: Long jump
D: Javelin

If you would like to use your 50:50 please turn to page 252
Turn to the answer section on page 260 to find out if you've won $125,000!

31

Which Shakespeare play is set in the forest of Arden?

- A: As You Like It
- B: Twelfth Night
- C: Measure For Measure
- D: A Midsummer Night's Dream

32

The Victoria Falls separate Zimbabwe from which other country?

- A: Swaziland
- B: Zambia
- C: Botswana
- D: Mozambique

33

Which metal is obtained from bauxite?

- A: Aluminium
- B: Sodium
- C: Copper
- D: Tin

34

Which European language is officially used in Madagascar?

- A: French
- B: Spanish
- C: Dutch
- D: Italian

35

What was the profession of John Maynard Keynes?

- A: Clergyman
- B: Economist
- C: Mountaineer
- D: Soldier

If you would like to use your 50:50 please turn to page 252
Turn to the answer section on page 260 to find out if you've won $125,000!

36

A Monégasque is a native of which country?

- A: Mongolia
- B: Madagascar
- C: Monaco
- D: Malta

37

The dodo was native to which island?

- A: Mauritius
- B: Borneo
- C: Zanzibar
- D: Madagascar

38

The world's second largest barrier reef is off the coast of which country?

- A: Belize
- B: Kenya
- C: Dominican Republic
- D: Papua New Guinea

39

Which of these world leaders died in 1953?

- A: Winston Churchill
- B: Josef Stalin
- C: Franklin D. Roosevelt
- D: Konrad Adenauer

40

At the Burke and Wills expedition's depot 65, what simple message was cut into the trunk of a coolibah tree on the banks of Cooper's Creek?

- A: Head south
- B: Dig
- C: SOS
- D: Water here

If you would like to use your 50:50 please turn to page 252
Turn to the answer section on page 260 to find out if you've won $125,000!

41

What does 'stegosaurus' mean?

- A: Spiny lizard
- B: Roof lizard
- C: Claw lizard
- D: Flat lizard

42

Which Australian federal electorate is the world's largest in area?

- A: Capricornia
- B: Casey
- C: Corinella
- D: Kalgoorlie

If you would like to use your 50:50 please turn to page 252
Turn to the answer section on page 260 to find out if you've won $125,000!

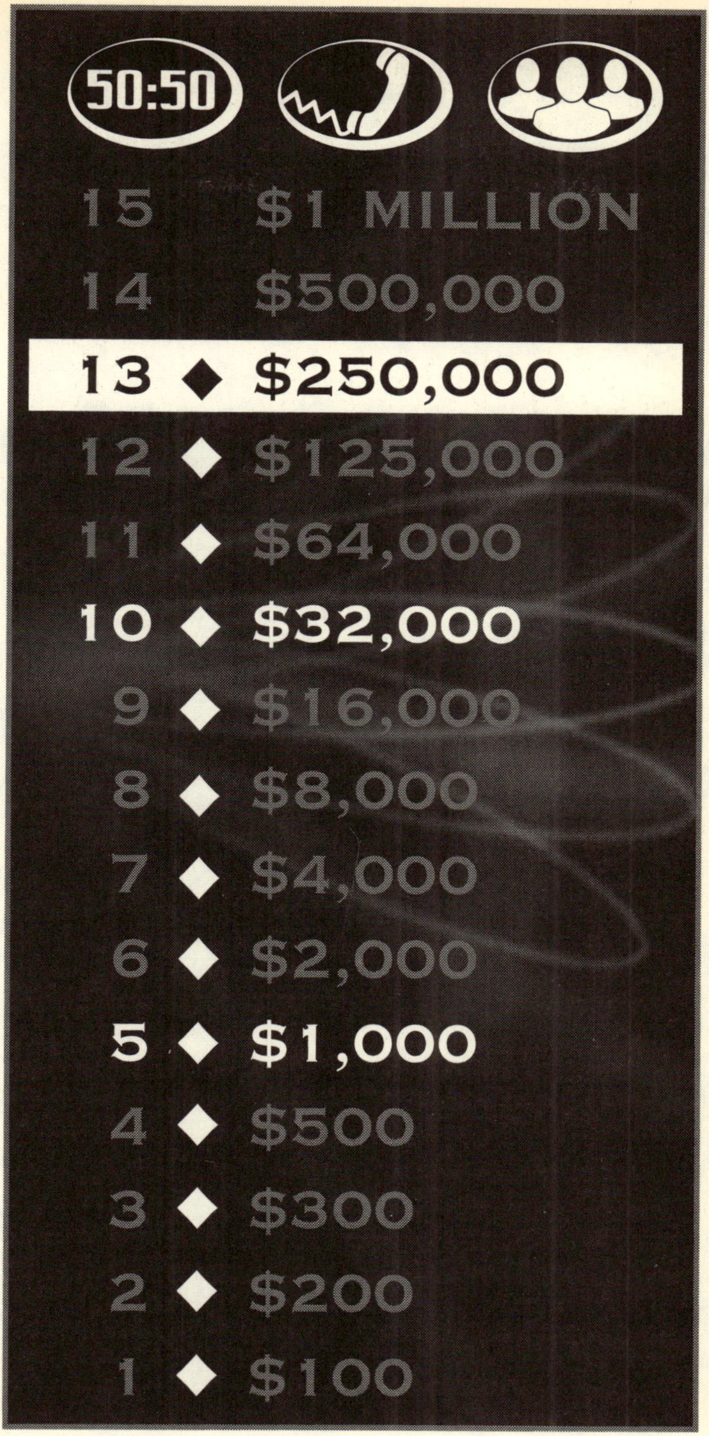
50:50
15 $1 MILLION
14 $500,000
13 ◆ $250,000
12 ◆ $125,000
11 ◆ $64,000
10 ◆ $32,000
9 ◆ $16,000
8 ◆ $8,000
7 ◆ $4,000
6 ◆ $2,000
5 ◆ $1,000
4 ◆ $500
3 ◆ $300
2 ◆ $200
1 ◆ $100

13 ◆ $250,000

1

In which two years did Australian tennis star Evonne Goolagong-Cawley win the Wimbledon ladies singles title?

A: 1970 & 1981
B: 1971 & 1980
C: 1972 & 1981
D: 1973 & 1980

2

Which was the first film to feature the on-screen pairing of Spencer Tracy and Katharine Hepburn?

A: Morning Glory
B: Adam's Rib
C: Guess Who's Coming to Dinner?
D: Woman of the Year

3

Who was awarded the Nobel Peace Prize in 1979?

A: Desmond Tutu
B: Amnesty International
C: The Dalai Lama
D: Mother Teresa of Calcutta

4

Which Australian artist painted the 'Half-Caste Bride' series?

A: Arthur Boyd
B: Albert Namatjira
C: Lloyd Rees
D: Brett Whiteley

5

Who wrote the music of the German national anthem?

A: Josef Haydn
B: Richard Wagner
C: Johannes Brahms
D: Ludwig van Beethoven

If you would like to use your 50:50 please turn to page 253
Turn to the answer section on page 261 to find out if you've won $250,000!

6

'View of Delft' is one of the best known works by which artist?

A: Van Dyck
B: Rembrandt
C: Van Eyck
D: Vermeer

7

Where is the largest volcano known to man?

A: Hawaii
B: Mars
C: Peru
D: Venus

8

In March 1965, who became the first person to walk in space?

A: Ed White
B: Vladimir Komarov
C: James McDivett
D: Alexei Leonov

9

In which year was Marie Antoinette, the wife of Louis XVI of France, executed?

A: 1791
B: 1793
C: 1795
D: 1797

10

Which country has a new parliament building known as the 'Beehive'?

A: England
B: Canada
C: Ireland
D: New Zealand

If you would like to use your 50:50 please turn to page 253
Turn to the answer section on page 261 to find out if you've won $250,000!

11

What nationality was the astronomer Copernicus?

- A: Swedish
- B: Dutch
- C: Polish
- D: Greek

12

Who was the first Republican president of the United States?

- A: John Adams
- B: Abraham Lincoln
- C: Grover Cleveland
- D: Theodore Roosevelt

13

As the crow flies, which mainland Australian state capital is furthest from Uluru?

- A: Brisbane
- B: Melbourne
- C: Sydney
- D: Perth

14

The king and crown prince of which country were assassinated on the same day in 1908?

- A: Italy
- B: Portugal
- C: Greece
- D: Romania

15

Which of these waves have the shortest wavelength?

- A: Gamma rays
- B: X-rays
- C: Ultraviolet waves
- D: Infra-red waves

If you would like to use your 50:50 please turn to page 253
Turn to the answer section on page 261 to find out if you've won $250,000!

16

How many satellites has the planet Uranus?

- A: Nine
- B: Eleven
- C: Thirteen
- D: Fifteen

17

With which of these composers did the female French novelist George Sand have an affair?

- A: Bizet
- B: Berlioz
- C: Chopin
- D: Debussy

18

Which knight of the Round Table fought a mysterious Green Knight?

- A: Sir Lancelot
- B: Sir Gawain
- C: Sir Percival
- D: Sir Galahad

19

Which other Victorian city hosted Olympic events during the Melbourne Olympics?

- A: Ballarat
- B: Bendigo
- C: Geelong
- D: Shepparton

20

Gariwerd is the Aboriginal name for which Australian mountain range?

- A: Blue Mountains
- B: Flinders Ranges
- C: Grampians
- D: Macdonnell Ranges

If you would like to use your 50:50 please turn to page 253
Turn to the answer section on page 261 to find out if you've won $250,000!

21

In Greek mythology, Penelope was the faithful wife of which hero?

- A: Jason
- B: Achilles
- C: Odysseus
- D: Hector

22

Which Australian novelist published 'The Timeless Land' in 1941?

- A: Ivan Southall
- B: Christina Stead
- C: Lennie Lower
- D: Eleanor Dark

23

Which of these leading Australian poets died in 2000?

- A: Judith Wright
- B: Kenneth Slessor
- C: Gwen Harwood
- D: Geoffrey Dutton

24

On which date in October 1929 was 'Black Thursday', the day the Wall Street Crash began?

- A: 24th
- B: 25th
- C: 28th
- D: 29th

25

At the 1976 Montreal Olympics, Australia's best result was a solitary silver medal won by whom?

- A: Michelle Ford
- B: Stephen Holland
- C: Men's coxed pairs
- D: Men's hockey team

If you would like to use your 50:50 please turn to page 253
Turn to the answer section on page 261 to find out if you've won $250,000!

26

In 1987, who became the first woman to be appointed a judge of the High Court?

A: Elizabeth Evatt
B: Roma Mitchell
C: Mary Gaudron
D: Pat O'Shane

27

Which high-profile Australian married Jessie Menzies in 1932?

A: Don Bradman
B: Frank Packer
C: Robert Menzies
D: Charles Kingsford-Smith

28

Which town was the site of the first European settlement in Western Australia?

A: Albany
B: Esperance
C: Bunbury
D: Fremantle

29

What is Labor leader Kim Beazley's middle name?

A: George
B: Christian
C: Francis
D: Edward

30

Published in 1981, Patrick White's autobiography is titled 'Flaws in the what'?

A: Glass
B: Mirror
C: Character
D: Pattern

If you would like to use your 50:50 please turn to page 253
Turn to the answer section on page 261 to find out if you've won $250,000!

31

Frank Lloyd Wright designed which famous New York building?

- A: UN Headquarters
- B: The Twin Towers
- C: Empire State Building
- D: Guggenheim Museum

32

Which of these Italian cities lies on the river Arno?

- A: Florence
- B: Milan
- C: Rome
- D: Venice

33

How many stars are there on the national flag of China?

- A: Four
- B: Five
- C: Six
- D: Seven

34

Who wrote the song 'I Will Always Love You', a hit in 1992 for Whitney Houston?

- A: Henry Mancini
- B: Burt Bacharach
- C: Don Black
- D: Dolly Parton

35

What was the name of the first US space shuttle?

- A: Discovery
- B: Columbia
- C: Challenger
- D: Atlantis

If you would like to use your 50:50 please turn to page 253
Turn to the answer section on page 261 to find out if you've won $250,000!

36

Who wrote the music for 'West Side Story'?

A: Stephen Sondheim
B: George Gershwin
C: Leonard Bernstein
D: Richard Rodgers

37

Which Formula One Grand Prix takes place at the Spa circuit?

A: German
B: Austrian
C: Belgian
D: Hungarian

38

What do the initials stand for in the name of the author H.G. Wells?

A: Horace George
B: Herbert George
C: Harold Gilbert
D: Henry Gilbert

If you would like to use your 50:50 please turn to page 253
Turn to the answer section on page 261 to find out if you've won $250,000!

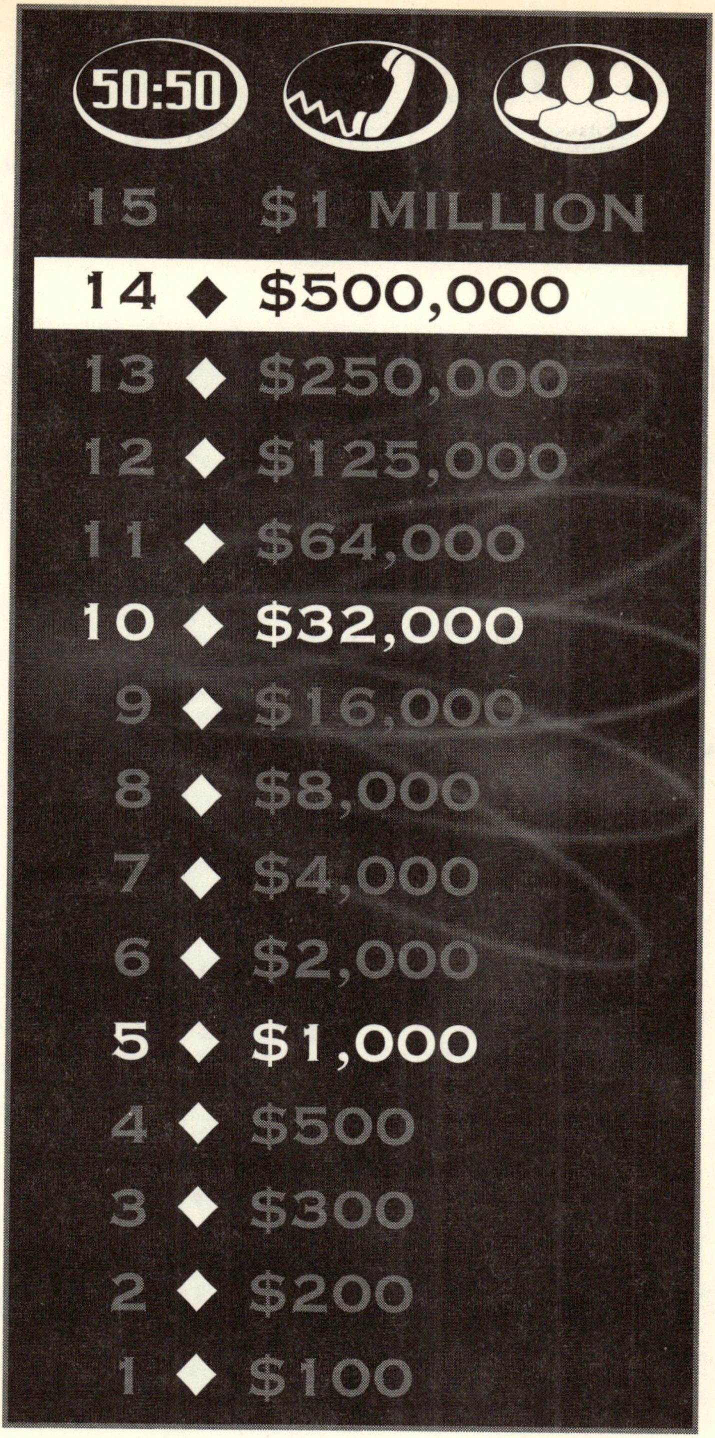
50:50
15 $1 MILLION
14 ◆ $500,000
13 ◆ $250,000
12 ◆ $125,000
11 ◆ $64,000
10 ◆ $32,000
9 ◆ $16,000
8 ◆ $8,000
7 ◆ $4,000
6 ◆ $2,000
5 ◆ $1,000
4 ◆ $500
3 ◆ $300
2 ◆ $200
1 ◆ $100

14 ◆ $500,000

1

The legendary 16th-century Portuguese shipwreck, believed buried beneath sand dunes on Victoria's west coast, is called the 'what' ship?

A: Ebony
B: Mahogany
C: Oak
D: Teak

2

Minsk, a city of the former Soviet Union, is now the capital of which country?

A: Belarus
B: Kazakhstan
C: Armenia
D: Lithuania

3

In which year were the first honours awards made under the Order of Australia?

A: 1973
B: 1974
C: 1975
D: 1976

4

What is the name of the highest waterfall in North America?

A: Niagara
B: Horseshoe
C: Yosemite
D: Ribbon

5

What name did the artist Michelangelo Merisi adopt?

A: Correggio
B: Titian
C: Botticelli
D: Caravaggio

If you would like to use your 50:50 please turn to page 253
Turn to the answer section on page 261 to find out if you've won $500,000!

6

Australian Florence Austral was famous in which stage profession?

- A: Acting
- B: Ballet
- C: Cabaret
- D: Opera

7

Which of the following towns is located north of the Tropic of Capricorn?

- A: Winton
- B: Alice Springs
- C: Carnarvon
- D: Roma

8

Who composed the opera 'Lohengrin'?

- A: Mahler
- B: Puccini
- C: Wagner
- D: Rossini

9

After the allied surrender in February 1942, which general made a daring escape from Singapore?

- A: Gordon Bennett
- B: Thomas Blamey
- C: Leslie Morshead
- D: Ian Campbell

10

From which author's work did scientists take the word 'quark'?

- A: Lewis Carroll
- B: Edward Lear
- C: James Joyce
- D: Aldous Huxley

If you would like to use your 50:50 please turn to page 253
Turn to the answer section on page 261 to find out if you've won $500,000!

11

Which planet has a moon called Larissa?

- A: Jupiter
- B: Saturn
- C: Uranus
- D: Neptune

12

What colour is the mineral malachite?

- A: Black
- B: White
- C: Purple
- D: Green

13

Which aviator was at the centre of the 1929 'Coffee Royal' incident?

- A: Charles Kingsford-Smith
- B: Bert Hinkler
- C: Arthur Butler
- D: Amelia Earhart

14

In the early 1890s in which South American country did William Lane establish his short-lived utopian community?

- A: Uruguay
- B: Argentina
- C: Paraguay
- D: Chile

15

Which family fought the Earp brothers at the OK Corral?

- A: The Clantons
- B: The Clintons
- C: The Cliftons
- D: The Graftons

If you would like to use your 50:50 please turn to page 253
Turn to the answer section on page 261 to find out if you've won $500,000!

16

The Somerset Maugham novel 'The Moon and Sixpence' is set on which island?

- A: Cuba
- B: Isle of Wight
- C: Madeira
- D: Tahiti

17

Which of these elements is contained in a strip-lighting tube?

- A: Mercury
- B: Cobalt
- C: Sodium
- D: Carbon

18

What is the name of the largest asteroid in the Solar System?

- A: Ceres
- B: Pallas
- C: Hygeia
- D: Vesta

19

Which of these novels is not part of Henry Handel Richardson's trilogy 'The Fortunes of Richard Mahony'?

- A: Australia Felix
- B: Maurice Guest
- C: Ultima Thule
- D: The Way Home

20

On which Australian islands did British scientists first explode an atomic bomb in 1952?

- A: Cartier
- B: Cocos
- C: Monte Bello
- D: Muiron

If you would like to use your 50:50 please turn to page 253
Turn to the answer section on page 261 to find out if you've won $500,000!

21

With only two survivors, what iron clipper was wrecked near Cape Otway off Victoria's coast in 1878?

A: Lake Illawarra
B: Lady Bird
C: Loch Ard
D: Loch Maree

22

Yellowstone National Park is mainly in which US state?

A: North Dakota
B: Kansas
C: Wyoming
D: Nevada

23

Which of these was first to be introduced in 1960s-Australia?

A: National Service
B: Four-digit postcodes
C: Contraceptive pill
D: Decimal currency

24

Who published several Australian children's books featuring the character Digit Dick?

A: Martin Boyd
B: Leslie Rees
C: Louis Stone
D: Francis Webb

25

To which bird family does the brolga belong?

A: Heron
B: Ibis
C: Stork
D: Crane

If you would like to use your 50:50 please turn to page 253
Turn to the answer section on page 261 to find out if you've won $500,000!

26

Ginger Rogers won a Best Actress Oscar for the film 'Kitty Foyle', released in which year?

- A: 1934
- B: 1936
- C: 1938
- D: 1940

27

Which German author wrote 'All Quiet on the Western Front'?

- A: Rainer Maria Rilke
- B: Bertolt Brecht
- C: Günter Grass
- D: Erich Maria Remarque

28

In which century was the artist Michelangelo born?

- A: 13th
- B: 14th
- C: 15th
- D: 16th

29

Which of these wine bottles is about six times the standard size?

- A: Methuselah
- B: Rehoboam
- C: Salmanazar
- D: Balthazar

30

In which month in 1952 did Queen Elizabeth II accede to the throne?

- A: January
- B: February
- C: March
- D: April

If you would like to use your 50:50 please turn to page 253
Turn to the answer section on page 261 to find out if you've won $500,000!

14 ◆ $500,000

31

Which Moscow building was the headquarters of the Parliament of the Russian Republic?

- A: The White House
- B: The Red Citadel
- C: The Winter Palace
- D: The Dome

32

What is the official language of Guyana?

- A: Spanish
- B: Portuguese
- C: French
- D: English

33

Which Australian cricketer was born the same year that the Smith brothers became the first to fly from England to Australia?

- A: Don Bradman
- B: Keith Miller
- C: Bill Ponsford
- D: Bill Woodfull

34

Who was the second Roman emperor?

- A: Claudius
- B: Tiberius
- C: Nero
- D: Augustus

If you would like to use your 50:50 please turn to page 253
Turn to the answer section on page 261 to find out if you've won $500,000!

50:50

15 ◆ $1 MILLION

14 ◆ $500,000

13 ◆ $250,000

12 ◆ $125,000

11 ◆ $64,000

10 ◆ $32,000

9 ◆ $16,000

8 ◆ $8,000

7 ◆ $4,000

6 ◆ $2,000

5 ◆ $1,000

4 ◆ $500

3 ◆ $300

2 ◆ $200

1 ◆ $100

15 ◆ $1,000,000

1

The largest of the great salt lakes of South Australia, Lake Eyre North is connected to Lake Eyre South by which usually dry channel?

- A: Stuart
- B: Torrens
- C: Gawler
- D: Goyder

2

Which Australian architect designed the $160 million Yulara tourist resort at Uluru?

- A: Richard Thorp
- B: Daryl Jackson
- C: Glen Murcutt
- D: Philip Cox

3

The Four Noble Truths are central to which religion?

- A: Buddhism
- B: Islam
- C: Hinduism
- D: Judaism

4

What electoral reform was introduced in South Australia and Victoria in 1856?

- A: Secret ballot
- B: Preferential voting
- C: Compulsory voting
- D: Postal voting

5

Which bushranger had the nickname 'Captain Melville'?

- A: Frederick Ward
- B: Frank McCallum
- C: Martin Cash
- D: John Donahoe

If you would like to use your 50:50 please turn to page 254
Turn to the answer section on page 261 to find out if you've won $1,000,000!

6

In which year was the anniversary of Australia's settlement, now called Australia Day, first celebrated as a public holiday?

- A: 1818
- B: 1838
- C: 1888
- D: 1938

7

What is the title of the third part of T.S. Eliot's poem 'The Waste Land'?

- A: A Game of Chess
- B: Death by Water
- C: What the Thunder Said
- D: The Fire Sermon

8

What is 'phylloxera'?

- A: A lung infection
- B: An insect
- C: A shrub
- D: Green pigment

9

In area, which of these Australian national parks is the largest?

- A: Lakefield, Qld
- B: Rudall River, WA
- C: Southwest, Tas
- D: Witjira, SA

10

The fall in pitch of a vehicle's siren as it passes is associated with which scientist?

- A: Corioli
- B: Newton
- C: Doppler
- D: Hooke

If you would like to use your 50:50 please turn to page 254
Turn to the answer section on page 261 to find out if you've won $1,000,000!

11

Sir Seretse Khama was the first president of which country?

A: Botswana
B: Tanzania
C: Ghana
D: Zambia

12

Which decimal number is equal to the binary number 10?

A: Ten
B: Two
C: One
D: Three

13

Which star type has the hottest surface temperature?

A: White
B: Red
C: Blue
D: Yellow

14

Which New South Wales governor's achievements in astronomy brought him greater fame than his military or vice-regal careers?

A: Bourke
B: Fitzroy
C: Darling
D: Brisbane

15

Which of these colours does not appear on the national flag of Lithuania?

A: Blue
B: Yellow
C: Red
D: Green

If you would like to use your 50:50 please turn to page 254
Turn to the answer section on page 261 to find out if you've won $1,000,000!

16

The first regular census in New South Wales was taken in which year?

- A: 1826
- B: 1828
- C: 1836
- D: 1840

17

Linking the eastern states to Perth, in which year was the Trans-Australian Railway completed?

- A: 1915
- B: 1916
- C: 1917
- D: 1918

18

Which of these is not a mineral used on the Mohs scale of hardness?

- A: Orthoclase
- B: Apatite
- C: Graphite
- D: Gypsum

19

Which extensive tableland area's highest peaks are Round Mountain and Point Lookout?

- A: Kimberley
- B: Atherton
- C: New England
- D: Barkly

20

At the 1956 Melbourne Olympics, by what score did Hungary defeat the Soviet Union in the notorious abandoned 'bloodbath' water polo match?

- A: 4-0
- B: 4-1
- C: 4-2
- D: 4-3

If you would like to use your 50:50 please turn to page 254
Turn to the answer section on page 261 to find out if you've won $1,000,000!

21

Tasmania is larger in area than which of these European countries?

- A: Austria
- B: Greece
- C: Ireland
- D: Denmark

22

Which cartoon character made his screen debut in 1935?

- A: Porky Pig
- B: Popeye
- C: Pluto
- D: Bugs Bunny

23

Near which Victorian town was the huge Welcome Stranger gold nugget found in 1869?

- A: Avoca
- B: Bendigo
- C: Creswick
- D: Dunolly

24

What invention did Frederick Wolseley patent in Australia in 1877?

- A: Curved sail windmill
- B: Irrigation pump
- C: Sheep shearing machine
- D: Spun concrete

25

In which northern English town was navigator Captain Cook born in 1728?

- A: Marton-in-Cleveland
- B: Berwick-upon-Tweed
- C: Chester le-Street
- D: Stockton-on-Tees

If you would like to use your 50:50 please turn to page 254
Turn to the answer section on page 261 to find out if you've won $1,000,000!

26

Which of these Torres Strait islands is closest to the island of New Guinea?

- A: Boigu
- B: Moa
- C: Prince of Wales
- D: Thursday

27

What was the first name of L. Frank Baum, author of 'The Wonderful Wizard of Oz'?

- A: Linus
- B: Lyman
- C: Lionel
- D: Leon

28

In which year was Mahatma Gandhi assassinated?

- A: 1946
- B: 1947
- C: 1948
- D: 1949

29

Edward Whymper was the first man to climb which of these mountains?

- A: Matterhorn
- B: K2
- C: Olympus
- D: Eiger

30

Which of Henry VIII's wives was the widow of his elder brother Arthur?

- A: Catherine of Aragon
- B: Anne of Cleves
- C: Catherine Howard
- D: Catherine Parr

If you would like to use your 50:50 please turn to page 254
Turn to the answer section on page 261 to find out if you've won $1,000,000!

50:50

$100

1 options remaining are A & B
2 options remaining are A & D
3 options remaining are A & C
4 options remaining are A & D
5 options remaining are B & C
6 options remaining are A & C
7 options remaining are C & D
8 options remaining are A & B
9 options remaining are C & D
10 options remaining are B & C
11 options remaining are A & B
12 options remaining are A & B
13 options remaining are A & C
14 options remaining are C & D
15 options remaining are A & C
16 options remaining are B & C
17 options remaining are A & B
18 options remaining are B & D
19 options remaining are A & D
20 options remaining are A & B
21 options remaining are A & D
22 options remaining are B & D
23 options remaining are B & D
24 options remaining are A & C
25 options remaining are B & C
26 options remaining are A & C
27 options remaining are A & C
28 options remaining are A & C
29 options remaining are A & D
30 options remaining are C & D
31 options remaining are C & D
32 options remaining are A & C
33 options remaining are B & D
34 options remaining are A & B
35 options remaining are B & D
36 options remaining are B & D
37 options remaining are B & D
38 options remaining are B & D
39 options remaining are A & C
40 options remaining are A & C
41 options remaining are A & B
42 options remaining are A & B
43 options remaining are B & D
44 options remaining are B & C
45 options remaining are C & D
46 options remaining are A & B
47 options remaining are A & C
48 options remaining are B & D
49 options remaining are B & D
50 options remaining are A & C
51 options remaining are A & B
52 options remaining are A & B
53 options remaining are B & D
54 options remaining are A & C
55 options remaining are C & D
56 options remaining are A & D
57 options remaining are A & B
58 options remaining are B & D
59 options remaining are A & C
60 options remaining are A & C
61 options remaining are A & C
62 options remaining are A & C
63 options remaining are A & D
64 options remaining are A & D
65 options remaining are C & D
66 options remaining are A & D
67 options remaining are B & D
68 options remaining are B & C
69 options remaining are B & D
70 options remaining are B & C
71 options remaining are B & D
72 options remaining are C & D
73 options remaining are A & B
74 options remaining are C & D

75 options remaining are A & C
76 options remaining are A & B
77 options remaining are A & D
78 options remaining are A & C
79 options remaining are C & D
80 options remaining are A & C
81 options remaining are A & B
82 options remaining are A & C
83 options remaining are A & B
84 options remaining are B & C
85 options remaining are C & D
86 options remaining are B & C
87 options remaining are C & D
88 options remaining are A & D
89 options remaining are B & C
90 options remaining are C & D
91 options remaining are B & D
92 options remaining are B & D
93 options remaining are B & C
94 options remaining are A & B
95 options remaining are A & B
96 options remaining are B & D
97 options remaining are C & D
98 options remaining are B & D
99 options remaining are A & D
100 options remaining are B & C
101 options remaining are B & C
102 options remaining are A & B
103 options remaining are B & C
104 options remaining are C & D
105 options remaining are A & C
106 options remaining are A & B
107 options remaining are B & C
108 options remaining are B & C
109 options remaining are A & D
110 options remaining are A & C

$200

1 options remaining are A & C
2 options remaining are A & B
3 options remaining are A & B
4 options remaining are B & D
5 options remaining are A & D
6 options remaining are A & B
7 options remaining are A & C
8 options remaining are C & D
9 options remaining are A & D
10 options remaining are C & D
11 options remaining are A & D
12 options remaining are A & D
13 options remaining are C & D
14 options remaining are B & C
15 options remaining are B & C
16 options remaining are A & D
17 options remaining are A & C
18 options remaining are A & D
19 options remaining are A & D
20 options remaining are C & D
21 options remaining are A & C
22 options remaining are B & D
23 options remaining are A & C
24 options remaining are A & B
25 options remaining are A & C
26 options remaining are A & C
27 options remaining are A & B
28 options remaining are A & B
29 options remaining are B & C
30 options remaining are A & D
31 options remaining are B & C
32 options remaining are A & C
33 options remaining are A & B
34 options remaining are B & C
35 options remaining are A & C
36 options remaining are A & D
37 options remaining are B & D
38 options remaining are A & D
39 options remaining are A & C
40 options remaining are A & B
41 options remaining are A & D
42 options remaining are A & C

43 options remaining are A & D
44 options remaining are A & C
45 options remaining are A & B
46 options remaining are A & B
47 options remaining are B & D
48 options remaining are A & C
49 options remaining are A & D
50 options remaining are B & D
51 options remaining are A & D
52 options remaining are B & C
53 options remaining are C & D
54 options remaining are A & C
55 options remaining are A & D
56 options remaining are A & D
57 options remaining are A & B
58 options remaining are B & C
59 options remaining are C & D
60 options remaining are A & B
61 options remaining are A & C
62 options remaining are A & D
63 options remaining are C & D
64 options remaining are B & D
65 options remaining are A & B
66 options remaining are B & D
67 options remaining are A & D
68 options remaining are B & D
69 options remaining are B & C
70 options remaining are A & B
71 options remaining are A & C
72 options remaining are B & D
73 options remaining are C & D
74 options remaining are A & C
75 options remaining are A & D
76 options remaining are A & C
77 options remaining are A & B
78 options remaining are C & D
79 options remaining are A & B
80 options remaining are C & D
81 options remaining are A & C
82 options remaining are B & D
83 options remaining are C & D
84 options remaining are A & C
85 options remaining are A & B
86 options remaining are C & D
87 options remaining are B & C
88 options remaining are B & C
89 options remaining are B & D
90 options remaining are A & D
91 options remaining are B & D
92 options remaining are A & C
93 options remaining are A & D
94 options remaining are B & D
95 options remaining are B & D
96 options remaining are B & C
97 options remaining are A & C
98 options remaining are A & C

$300

1 options remaining are B & C
2 options remaining are A & D
3 options remaining are B & D
4 options remaining are A & C
5 options remaining are A & B
6 options remaining are A & B
7 options remaining are A & D
8 options remaining are A & D
9 options remaining are A & D
10 options remaining are A & D
11 options remaining are A & D
12 options remaining are A & D
13 options remaining are A & D
14 options remaining are A & C
15 options remaining are A & D
16 options remaining are A & C
17 options remaining are A & B
18 options remaining are A & D
19 options remaining are A & B
20 options remaining are A & D
21 options remaining are A & D
22 options remaining are A & D
23 options remaining are C & D
24 options remaining are A & B
25 options remaining are B & C
26 options remaining are C & D
27 options remaining are B & C
28 options remaining are A & B
29 options remaining are A & D
30 options remaining are A & B
31 options remaining are B & D
32 options remaining are A & C
33 options remaining are A & D
34 options remaining are B & D
35 options remaining are C & D
36 options remaining are B & C
37 options remaining are A & D
38 options remaining are C & D
39 options remaining are B & C
40 options remaining are A & B
41 options remaining are B & D
42 options remaining are B & D
43 options remaining are B & C
44 options remaining are C & D
45 options remaining are B & C
46 options remaining are B & D
47 options remaining are A & D
48 options remaining are B & C
49 options remaining are B & D
50 options remaining are A & D
51 options remaining are B & D
52 options remaining are A & D
53 options remaining are C & D
54 options remaining are A & D
55 options remaining are A & C
56 options remaining are A & C
57 options remaining are A & B
58 options remaining are A & B
59 options remaining are A & D
60 options remaining are A & D
61 options remaining are B & D
62 options remaining are A & B
63 options remaining are A & C
64 options remaining are A & D
65 options remaining are B & D
66 options remaining are C & D
67 options remaining are B & D
68 options remaining are B & C
69 options remaining are A & C
70 options remaining are A & C
71 options remaining are A & D
72 options remaining are B & C
73 options remaining are B & C
74 options remaining are A & B
75 options remaining are B & C
76 options remaining are B & D
77 options remaining are A & C
78 options remaining are C & D
79 options remaining are A & C
80 options remaining are A & B
81 options remaining are A & C
82 options remaining are A & C
83 options remaining are A & C
84 options remaining are A & C

85 options remaining are A & B
86 options remaining are A & B
87 options remaining are A & C
88 options remaining are C & D
89 options remaining are A & B
90 options remaining are B & C
91 options remaining are C & D
92 options remaining are B & D
93 options remaining are C & D
94 options remaining are C & D

$500

1 options remaining are A & B
2 options remaining are A & D
3 options remaining are B & D
4 options remaining are B & C
5 options remaining are C & D
6 options remaining are A & C
7 options remaining are A & C
8 options remaining are A & B
9 options remaining are B & C
10 options remaining are A & B
11 options remaining are C & D
12 options remaining are A & D
13 options remaining are A & B
14 options remaining are A & C
15 options remaining are A & B
16 options remaining are A & C
17 options remaining are C & D
18 options remaining are A & C
19 options remaining are A & C
20 options remaining are C & D
21 options remaining are A & B
22 options remaining are B & D
23 options remaining are B & D
24 options remaining are A & B
25 options remaining are A & D
26 options remaining are B & D
27 options remaining are A & B
28 options remaining are A & D
29 options remaining are A & B
30 options remaining are B & D
31 options remaining are A & D
32 options remaining are A & D
33 options remaining are B & D
34 options remaining are A & D
35 options remaining are C & D
36 options remaining are B & C
37 options remaining are B & D
38 options remaining are A & B
39 options remaining are A & B
40 options remaining are A & C
41 options remaining are A & D
42 options remaining are C & D

43 options remaining are A & D
44 options remaining are B & C
45 options remaining are A & D
46 options remaining are A & C
47 options remaining are A & D
48 options remaining are A & C
49 options remaining are A & C
50 options remaining are A & B
51 options remaining are B & D
52 options remaining are A & C
53 options remaining are C & D
54 options remaining are B & C
55 options remaining are B & D
56 options remaining are A & D
57 options remaining are B & C
58 options remaining are A & C
59 options remaining are B & C
60 options remaining are A & D
61 options remaining are B & C
62 options remaining are C & D
63 options remaining are C & D
64 options remaining are A & D
65 options remaining are A & D
66 options remaining are A & D
67 options remaining are A & B
68 options remaining are B & D
69 options remaining are A & B
70 options remaining are A & C
71 options remaining are C & D
72 options remaining are A & C
73 options remaining are C & D
74 options remaining are B & C
75 options remaining are B & D
76 options remaining are B & D
77 options remaining are B & D
78 options remaining are A & D
79 options remaining are A & D
80 options remaining are A & D
81 options remaining are C & D
82 options remaining are A & D
83 options remaining are A & C
84 options remaining are B & D
85 options remaining are A & C
86 options remaining are C & D
87 options remaining are A & D
88 options remaining are A & C
89 options remaining are A & D
90 options remaining are B & C

$1,000

1 options remaining are A & C
2 options remaining are A & B
3 options remaining are A & C
4 options remaining are A & B
5 options remaining are B & D
6 options remaining are A & D
7 options remaining are B & D
8 options remaining are A & C
9 options remaining are A & B
10 options remaining are B & C
11 options remaining are B & D
12 options remaining are C & D
13 options remaining are C & D
14 options remaining are A & C
15 options remaining are A & C
16 options remaining are B & D
17 options remaining are A & C
18 options remaining are A & B
19 options remaining are C & D
20 options remaining are A & C
21 options remaining are B & C
22 options remaining are B & D
23 options remaining are A & C
24 options remaining are A & B
25 options remaining are A & D
26 options remaining are B & D
27 options remaining are A & C
28 options remaining are A & C
29 options remaining are B & C
30 options remaining are B & D
31 options remaining are B & C
32 options remaining are A & B
33 options remaining are A & C
34 options remaining are C & D
35 options remaining are A & D
36 options remaining are C & D
37 options remaining are A & D
38 options remaining are A & D
39 options remaining are B & D
40 options remaining are A & B
41 options remaining are C & D
42 options remaining are A & D
43 options remaining are C & D
44 options remaining are A & D
45 options remaining are A & D
46 options remaining are A & D
47 options remaining are A & C
48 options remaining are A & B
49 options remaining are B & C
50 options remaining are C & D
51 options remaining are C & D
52 options remaining are A & B
53 options remaining are A & D
54 options remaining are A & B
55 options remaining are B & C
56 options remaining are A & D
57 options remaining are A & D
58 options remaining are A & B
59 options remaining are B & D
60 options remaining are A & C
61 options remaining are B & C
62 options remaining are A & C
63 options remaining are A & C
64 options remaining are A & D
65 options remaining are A & B
66 options remaining are A & D
67 options remaining are A & B
68 options remaining are B & D
69 options remaining are A & C
70 options remaining are A & D
71 options remaining are A & B
72 options remaining are A & D
73 options remaining are A & D
74 options remaining are A & C
75 options remaining are B & D
76 options remaining are A & D
77 options remaining are B & D
78 options remaining are A & B
79 options remaining are A & C
80 options remaining are B & D
81 options remaining are A & C
82 options remaining are B & D
83 options remaining are C & D
84 options remaining are A & D

85 options remaining are A & D
86 options remaining are B & D

$2,000

1 options remaining are A & C
2 options remaining are A & D
3 options remaining are A & D
4 options remaining are A & B
5 options remaining are C & D
6 options remaining are C & D
7 options remaining are A & B
8 options remaining are C & D
9 options remaining are B & D
10 options remaining are A & B
11 options remaining are A & D
12 options remaining are B & D
13 options remaining are B & C
14 options remaining are A & C
15 options remaining are A & D
16 options remaining are A & D
17 options remaining are A & C
18 options remaining are A & C
19 options remaining are B & C
20 options remaining are B & D
21 options remaining are C & D
22 options remaining are A & D
23 options remaining are B & D
24 options remaining are A & C
25 options remaining are A & D
26 options remaining are B & C
27 options remaining are C & D
28 options remaining are A & B
29 options remaining are A & C
30 options remaining are A & D
31 options remaining are A & D
32 options remaining are C & D
33 options remaining are A & D
34 options remaining are B & C
35 options remaining are A & B
36 options remaining are A & B
37 options remaining are B & D
38 options remaining are B & C
39 options remaining are C & D
40 options remaining are A & B
41 options remaining are C & D
42 options remaining are B & C

43 options remaining are A & D
44 options remaining are B & D
45 options remaining are B & D
46 options remaining are B & C
47 options remaining are C & D
48 options remaining are B & D
49 options remaining are A & D
50 options remaining are A & C
51 options remaining are B & D
52 options remaining are A & B
53 options remaining are A & B
54 options remaining are B & C
55 options remaining are A & B
56 options remaining are A & B
57 options remaining are C & D
58 options remaining are A & D
59 options remaining are B & D
60 options remaining are A & D
61 options remaining are C & D
62 options remaining are C & D
63 options remaining are A & D
64 options remaining are B & D
65 options remaining are A & C
66 options remaining are C & D
67 options remaining are A & D
68 options remaining are B & D
69 options remaining are B & D
70 options remaining are C & D
71 options remaining are A & C
72 options remaining are C & D
73 options remaining are A & B
74 options remaining are A & D

$4,000

1 options remaining are A & C
2 options remaining are A & C
3 options remaining are A & B
4 options remaining are A & C
5 options remaining are C & D
6 options remaining are A & C
7 options remaining are A & D
8 options remaining are A & D
9 options remaining are C & D
10 options remaining are A & B
11 options remaining are A & C
12 options remaining are A & B
13 options remaining are A & C
14 options remaining are A & B
15 options remaining are A & D
16 options remaining are A & B
17 options remaining are B & D
18 options remaining are A & B
19 options remaining are B & D
20 options remaining are A & D
21 options remaining are A & B
22 options remaining are A & B
23 options remaining are A & D
24 options remaining are A & D
25 options remaining are A & D
26 options remaining are A & B
27 options remaining are A & B
28 options remaining are B & D
29 options remaining are C & D
30 options remaining are A & B
31 options remaining are A & D
32 options remaining are A & D
33 options remaining are B & C
34 options remaining are A & B
35 options remaining are A & B
36 options remaining are A & B
37 options remaining are C & D
38 options remaining are A & C
39 options remaining are B & D
40 options remaining are B & D
41 options remaining are A & D
42 options remaining are B & C

43 options remaining are B & D
44 options remaining are A & C
45 options remaining are A & D
46 options remaining are C & D
47 options remaining are A & D
48 options remaining are A & B
49 options remaining are A & D
50 options remaining are A & B
51 options remaining are B & D
52 options remaining are A & D
53 options remaining are B & C
54 options remaining are A & B
55 options remaining are B & C
56 options remaining are B & C
57 options remaining are C & D
58 options remaining are B & C
59 options remaining are B & C
60 options remaining are C & D
61 options remaining are B & D
62 options remaining are B & D
63 options remaining are B & D
64 options remaining are B & D
65 options remaining are C & D
66 options remaining are A & B
67 options remaining are A & C
68 options remaining are A & C
69 options remaining are B & D
70 options remaining are B & D

$8,000

1 options remaining are A & B
2 options remaining are C & D
3 options remaining are A & D
4 options remaining are A & C
5 options remaining are A & D
6 options remaining are C & D
7 options remaining are A & D
8 options remaining are A & B
9 options remaining are A & C
10 options remaining are A & C
11 options remaining are A & D
12 options remaining are B & D
13 options remaining are B & D
14 options remaining are A & B
15 options remaining are A & B
16 options remaining are C & D
17 options remaining are A & D
18 options remaining are A & D
19 options remaining are A & D
20 options remaining are A & D
21 options remaining are A & B
22 options remaining are A & C
23 options remaining are A & D
24 options remaining are B & C
25 options remaining are B & C
26 options remaining are B & C
27 options remaining are A & B
28 options remaining are B & D
29 options remaining are B & C
30 options remaining are C & D
31 options remaining are A & C
32 options remaining are B & C
33 options remaining are A & C
34 options remaining are A & C
35 options remaining are B & C
36 options remaining are A & C
37 options remaining are A & B
38 options remaining are A & D
39 options remaining are A & D
40 options remaining are B & D
41 options remaining are B & D
42 options remaining are B & D

43 options remaining are A & C
44 options remaining are C & D
45 options remaining are A & D
46 options remaining are A & C
47 options remaining are A & B
48 options remaining are A & C
49 options remaining are A & B
50 options remaining are A & C
51 options remaining are C & D
52 options remaining are C & D
53 options remaining are A & D
54 options remaining are A & B
55 options remaining are A & C
56 options remaining are B & D
57 options remaining are A & D
58 options remaining are A & D
59 options remaining are A & B
60 options remaining are B & C
61 options remaining are C & D
62 options remaining are B & C
63 options remaining are A & B
64 options remaining are A & C
65 options remaining are A & C
66 options remaining are B & D

$16,000

1 options remaining are B & D
2 options remaining are A & C
3 options remaining are A & B
4 options remaining are B & C
5 options remaining are B & D
6 options remaining are B & C
7 options remaining are C & D
8 options remaining are A & B
9 options remaining are B & D
10 options remaining are A & B
11 options remaining are B & C
12 options remaining are A & B
13 options remaining are A & B
14 options remaining are A & C
15 options remaining are B & D
16 options remaining are B & C
17 options remaining are A & B
18 options remaining are A & D
19 options remaining are B & D
20 options remaining are A & D
21 options remaining are A & B
22 options remaining are C & D
23 options remaining are A & D
24 options remaining are A & B
25 options remaining are B & C
26 options remaining are C & D
27 options remaining are B & D
28 options remaining are C & D
29 options remaining are A & D
30 options remaining are A & D
31 options remaining are A & D
32 options remaining are A & D
33 options remaining are A & C
34 options remaining are C & D
35 options remaining are B & C
36 options remaining are C & D
37 options remaining are B & D
38 options remaining are A & D
39 options remaining are A & B
40 options remaining are A & B
41 options remaining are A & C
42 options remaining are A & B

43 options remaining are A & B
44 options remaining are C & D
45 options remaining are A & C
46 options remaining are B & C
47 options remaining are A & C
48 options remaining are A & D
49 options remaining are C & D
50 options remaining are C & D
51 options remaining are A & B
52 options remaining are B & C
53 options remaining are A & C
54 options remaining are C & D
55 options remaining are B & C
56 options remaining are A & C
57 options remaining are B & D
58 options remaining are C & D
59 options remaining are A & B
60 options remaining are B & D
61 options remaining are A & C
62 options remaining are A & D

$32,000

1 options remaining are B & C
2 options remaining are A & D
3 options remaining are A & B
4 options remaining are B & D
5 options remaining are B & D
6 options remaining are B & D
7 options remaining are A & D
8 options remaining are C & D
9 options remaining are A & D
10 options remaining are A & D
11 options remaining are A & B
12 options remaining are A & D
13 options remaining are A & C
14 options remaining are A & C
15 options remaining are A & C
16 options remaining are A & D
17 options remaining are C & D
18 options remaining are B & D
19 options remaining are A & B
20 options remaining are A & D
21 options remaining are C & D
22 options remaining are B & C
23 options remaining are A & B
24 options remaining are A & C
25 options remaining are A & D
26 options remaining are A & C
27 options remaining are A & B
28 options remaining are A & D
29 options remaining are A & B
30 options remaining are A & B
31 options remaining are C & D
32 options remaining are C & D
33 options remaining are A & B
34 options remaining are C & D
35 options remaining are A & C
36 options remaining are C & D
37 options remaining are A & B
38 options remaining are C & D
39 options remaining are A & D
40 options remaining are B & D
41 options remaining are B & D
42 options remaining are A & B

43 options remaining are A & B
44 options remaining are A & C
45 options remaining are B & C
46 options remaining are B & C
47 options remaining are C & D
48 options remaining are A & D
49 options remaining are A & D
50 options remaining are C & D
51 options remaining are A & B
52 options remaining are A & B
53 options remaining are C & D
54 options remaining are C & D
55 options remaining are B & C
56 options remaining are A & D
57 options remaining are A & C
58 options remaining are A & C

$64,000

1 options remaining are A & B
2 options remaining are A & D
3 options remaining are A & C
4 options remaining are B & C
5 options remaining are A & B
6 options remaining are B & C
7 options remaining are A & D
8 options remaining are A & D
9 options remaining are B & C
10 options remaining are A & C
11 options remaining are C & D
12 options remaining are A & B
13 options remaining are B & C
14 options remaining are A & C
15 options remaining are A & B
16 options remaining are C & D
17 options remaining are A & D
18 options remaining are B & C
19 options remaining are A & B
20 options remaining are B & C
21 options remaining are A & D
22 options remaining are A & B
23 options remaining are A & B
24 options remaining are B & D
25 options remaining are A & C
26 options remaining are A & B
27 options remaining are A & C
28 options remaining are C & D
29 options remaining are A & B
30 options remaining are A & B
31 options remaining are A & B
32 options remaining are C & D
33 options remaining are A & D
34 options remaining are B & C
35 options remaining are C & D
36 options remaining are A & D
37 options remaining are B & D
38 options remaining are A & B
39 options remaining are A & B
40 options remaining are B & D
41 options remaining are C & D
42 options remaining are B & C

43 options remaining are A & C
44 options remaining are B & D
45 options remaining are B & C
46 options remaining are B & C

$125,000

1 options remaining are A & C
2 options remaining are A & B
3 options remaining are B & C
4 options remaining are A & B
5 options remaining are A & B
6 options remaining are A & B
7 options remaining are A & C
8 options remaining are A & C
9 options remaining are B & D
10 options remaining are A & C
11 options remaining are A & C
12 options remaining are A & D
13 options remaining are A & D
14 options remaining are A & B
15 options remaining are A & C
16 options remaining are B & C
17 options remaining are A & D
18 options remaining are A & C
19 options remaining are C & D
20 options remaining are A & B
21 options remaining are C & D
22 options remaining are A & D
23 options remaining are B & D
24 options remaining are A & D
25 options remaining are A & B
26 options remaining are A & D
27 options remaining are B & D
28 options remaining are A & D
29 options remaining are A & D
30 options remaining are B & C
31 options remaining are A & D
32 options remaining are B & C
33 options remaining are A & C
34 options remaining are A & C
35 options remaining are A & B
36 options remaining are B & C
37 options remaining are A & D
38 options remaining are A & C
39 options remaining are B & D
40 options remaining are B & D
41 options remaining are A & B
42 options remaining are A & D

50:50

$250,000

1 options remaining are A & B
2 options remaining are A & D
3 options remaining are B & D
4 options remaining are A & C
5 options remaining are A & B
6 options remaining are C & D
7 options remaining are A & B
8 options remaining are B & D
9 options remaining are B & C
10 options remaining are A & D
11 options remaining are B & C
12 options remaining are B & C
13 options remaining are A & B
14 options remaining are B & D
15 options remaining are A & D
16 options remaining are B & D
17 options remaining are B & C
18 options remaining are B & C
19 options remaining are A & C
20 options remaining are C & D
21 options remaining are C & D
22 options remaining are A & D
23 options remaining are A & D
24 options remaining are A & D
25 options remaining are A & D
26 options remaining are C & D
27 options remaining are A & D
28 options remaining are A & D
29 options remaining are B & C
30 options remaining are A & B
31 options remaining are B & D
32 options remaining are A & C
33 options remaining are B & D
34 options remaining are C & D
35 options remaining are B & C
36 options remaining are A & C
37 options remaining are C & D
38 options remaining are B & D

$500,000

1 options remaining are B & C
2 options remaining are A & B
3 options remaining are C & D
4 options remaining are B & C
5 options remaining are B & D
6 options remaining are B & D
7 options remaining are A & D
8 options remaining are A & C
9 options remaining are A & B
10 options remaining are A & C
11 options remaining are B & D
12 options remaining are C & D
13 options remaining are A & C
14 options remaining are B & C
15 options remaining are A & C
16 options remaining are B & D
17 options remaining are A & C
18 options remaining are A & B
19 options remaining are A & B
20 options remaining are C & D
21 options remaining are C & D
22 options remaining are B & C
23 options remaining are B & C
24 options remaining are A & B
25 options remaining are C & D
26 options remaining are B & D
27 options remaining are A & D
28 options remaining are C & D
29 options remaining are A & B
30 options remaining are A & B
31 options remaining are A & C
32 options remaining are C & D
33 options remaining are B & C
34 options remaining are A & B

$1,000,000

1 options remaining are C & D
2 options remaining are A & D
3 options remaining are A & C
4 options remaining are A & C
5 options remaining are A & B
6 options remaining are B & C
7 options remaining are A & D
8 options remaining are B & D
9 options remaining are B & D
10 options remaining are A & C
11 options remaining are A & D
12 options remaining are A & B
13 options remaining are A & C
14 options remaining are B & D
15 options remaining are A & D
16 options remaining are B & D
17 options remaining are A & C
18 options remaining are C & D
19 options remaining are A & C
20 options remaining are A & D
21 options remaining are B & D
22 options remaining are A & B
23 options remaining are A & D
24 options remaining are B & C
25 options remaining are A & D
26 options remaining are A & B
27 options remaining are A & B
28 options remaining are B & C
29 options remaining are A & B
30 options remaining are A & B

Answers

$100

1	A	2	D	3	A	4	A	5	B
6	A	7	D	8	A	9	C	10	B
11	B	12	A	13	A	14	C	15	C
16	C	17	A	18	B	19	A	20	B
21	A	22	B	23	B	24	C	25	C
26	C	27	C	28	C	29	A	30	C
31	C	32	C	33	D	34	A	35	B
36	D	37	B	38	D	39	A	40	A
41	A	42	B	43	D	44	B	45	D
46	B	47	C	48	D	49	D	50	C
51	A	52	B	53	D	54	A	55	D
56	D	57	B	58	D	59	C	60	A
61	A	62	A	63	D	64	D	65	C
66	A	67	D	68	B	69	B	70	B
71	B	72	C	73	B	74	D	75	A
76	B	77	A	78	A	79	C	80	A
81	B	82	C	83	A	84	B	85	C
86	B	87	D	88	D	89	C	90	C
91	B	92	D	93	C	94	A	95	B
96	D	97	C	98	B	99	A	100	C
101	C	102	A	103	C	104	C	105	C
106	B	107	B	108	B	109	A	110	A

If you have won $100, well done! Turn to page 33 to play for $200!

$200

1	A	2	A	3	A	4	B	5	D
6	B	7	A	8	C	9	A	10	D
11	D	12	D	13	C	14	B	15	B
16	A	17	C	18	D	19	D	20	C
21	A	22	B	23	C	24	A	25	A
26	C	27	B	28	A	29	B	30	A
31	C	32	C	33	B	34	B	35	A
36	D	37	B	38	A	39	C	40	A
41	D	42	C	43	A	44	C	45	B
46	B	47	B	48	C	49	D	50	D

51 A	52 C	53 D	54 C	55 A
56 D	57 B	58 B	59 C	60 B
61 A	62 A	63 C	64 D	65 B
66 B	67 A	68 D	69 C	70 A
71 A	72 D	73 C	74 A	75 D
76 C	77 B	78 C	79 A	80 D
81 C	82 D	83 C	84 C	85 B
86 D	87 B	88 C	89 B	90 D
91 D	92 C	93 A	94 D	95 B
96 B	97 C	98 A		

If you have won $200, well done! Turn to page 55 to play for $300!

$300

1 B	2 D	3 D	4 C	5 A
6 A	7 D	8 D	9 A	10 D
11 D	12 D	13 D	14 A	15 D
16 C	17 B	18 A	19 B	20 D
21 A	22 D	23 C	24 B	25 B
26 C	27 C	28 B	29 A	30 B
31 B	32 C	33 D	34 D	35 D
36 C	37 D	38 C	39 C	40 A
41 B	42 D	43 B	44 C	45 C
46 B	47 A	48 B	49 D	50 D
51 B	52 D	53 C	54 A	55 C
56 A	57 B	58 A	59 D	60 D
61 B	62 B	63 A	64 A	65 D
66 C	67 B	68 B	69 A	70 A
71 A	72 C	73 B	74 A	75 B
76 B	77 A	78 C	79 A	80 B
81 A	82 A	83 A	84 C	85 A
86 B	87 A	88 C	89 B	90 B
91 D	92 D	93 C	94 C	

If you have won $300, well done! Turn to page 75 to play for $500!

ANSWERS

$500

1	B	2	D	3	B	4	C	5	D
6	C	7	A	8	A	9	C	10	B
11	D	12	D	13	B	14	A	15	B
16	C	17	D	18	A	19	A	20	C
21	A	22	B	23	D	24	B	25	D
26	D	27	A	28	A	29	B	30	D
31	D	32	A	33	D	34	D	35	C
36	C	37	D	38	A	39	B	40	A
41	A	42	D	43	A	44	B	45	D
46	A	47	A	48	C	49	C	50	B
51	B	52	C	53	C	54	B	55	B
56	A	57	B	58	C	59	B	60	D
61	B	62	C	63	C	64	D	65	D
66	D	67	B	68	B	69	A	70	C
71	D	72	C	73	D	74	C	75	D
76	D	77	B	78	A	79	D	80	A
81	C	82	D	83	C	84	B	85	C
86	C	87	D	88	C	89	D	90	C

If you have won $500, well done! Turn to page 95 to play for $1,000!

$1,000

1	A	2	A	3	C	4	B	5	B
6	A	7	B	8	C	9	A	10	B
11	D	12	D	13	C	14	A	15	A
16	B	17	A	18	B	19	C	20	C
21	B	22	B	23	C	24	A	25	A
26	D	27	C	28	A	29	B	30	D
31	C	32	B	33	C	34	C	35	A
36	D	37	A	38	A	39	D	40	A
41	D	42	D	43	D	44	D	45	D
46	D	47	A	48	B	49	B	50	C
51	C	52	B	53	A	54	A	55	C
56	A	57	A	58	B	59	B	60	C
61	B	62	C	63	A	64	D	65	B
66	A	67	B	68	B	69	C	70	D
71	B	72	A	73	A	74	C	75	B
76	A	77	B	78	B	79	C	80	B
81	A	82	B	83	C	84	D	85	A
86	D								

If you have won $1,000, well done! Turn to page 115 to play for $2,000!

ANSWERS

$2,000

1	C	2	A	3	A	4	A	5	D
6	D	7	A	8	C	9	D	10	B
11	D	12	B	13	B	14	C	15	A
16	A	17	A	18	A	19	C	20	B
21	D	22	A	23	D	24	C	25	A
26	B	27	D	28	B	29	C	30	A
31	D	32	C	33	D	34	C	35	A
36	B	37	B	38	C	39	C	40	B
41	C	42	B	43	A	44	B	45	B
46	B	47	D	48	D	49	A	50	A
51	B	52	B	53	A	54	C	55	B
56	A	57	D	58	D	59	D	60	A
61	D	62	C	63	A	64	B	65	C
66	D	67	D	68	B	69	B	70	C
71	C	72	C	73	A	74	A		

If you have won $2,000, well done! Turn to page 131 to play for $4,000!

$4,000

1	A	2	A	3	B	4	C	5	C
6	A	7	D	8	D	9	D	10	A
11	A	12	A	13	C	14	A	15	A
16	A	17	D	18	A	19	D	20	D
21	A	22	A	23	D	24	D	25	D
26	A	27	A	28	B	29	C	30	A
31	D	32	D	33	B	34	B	35	A
36	A	37	C	38	A	39	B	40	D
41	A	42	B	43	B	44	C	45	D
46	C	47	D	48	B	49	A	50	A
51	B	52	A	53	B	54	B	55	B
56	B	57	D	58	C	59	C	60	C
61	D	62	D	63	D	64	D	65	D
66	B	67	A	68	C	69	D	70	D

If you have won $4,000, well done! Turn to page 147 to play for $8,000!

$8,000

1	A	2	C	3	A	4	C	5	A
6	D	7	D	8	B	9	A	10	C
11	D	12	B	13	B	14	A	15	B
16	C	17	D	18	A	19	A	20	D
21	B	22	C	23	A	24	C	25	C
26	C	27	A	28	D	29	B	30	C
31	C	32	B	33	A	34	A	35	B
36	A	37	A	38	D	39	A	40	D
41	D	42	D	43	A	44	D	45	D
46	A	47	A	48	A	49	A	50	A
51	C	52	C	53	D	54	B	55	C
56	D	57	A	58	A	59	B	60	B
61	D	62	B	63	B	64	A	65	A
66	B								

If you have won $8,000, well done! Turn to page 163 to play for $16,000!

$16,000

1	B	2	A	3	A	4	C	5	D
6	C	7	C	8	A	9	D	10	B
11	C	12	A	13	A	14	C	15	B
16	B	17	A	18	D	19	B	20	D
21	A	22	C	23	D	24	B	25	B
26	D	27	B	28	C	29	A	30	D
31	A	32	D	33	A	34	C	35	B
36	D	37	D	38	A	39	B	40	B
41	A	42	A	43	B	44	D	45	C
46	C	47	C	48	A	49	C	50	D
51	A	52	B	53	C	54	D	55	C
56	C	57	D	58	C	59	A	60	D
61	C	62	A						

If you have won $16,000, well done! Turn to page 177 to play for $32,000!

ANSWERS

$32,000

1	B	2	A	3	A	4	B	5	B
6	B	7	D	8	C	9	A	10	A
11	A	12	D	13	C	14	A	15	C
16	D	17	D	18	D	19	B	20	D
21	C	22	B	23	A	24	C	25	D
26	C	27	A	28	D	29	A	30	B
31	D	32	C	33	A	34	C	35	C
36	D	37	A	38	C	39	A	40	B
41	B	42	A	43	B	44	C	45	C
46	C	47	D	48	A	49	A	50	D
51	B	52	B	53	C	54	C	55	C
56	D	57	A	58	C				

If you have won $32,000, well done! Turn to page 191 to play for $64,000!

$64,000

1	B	2	A	3	A	4	B	5	A
6	C	7	A	8	A	9	C	10	A
11	C	12	A	13	C	14	A	15	B
16	C	17	D	18	B	19	B	20	C
21	D	22	B	23	B	24	D	25	C
26	A	27	C	28	C	29	A	30	A
31	A	32	C	33	D	34	B	35	D
36	D	37	D	38	B	39	A	40	B
41	D	42	B	43	A	44	D	45	C
46	B								

If you have won $64,000, well done! Turn to page 203 to play for $125,000!

$125,000

1	A	2	A	3	C	4	B	5	B
6	B	7	C	8	C	9	B	10	A
11	A	12	D	13	D	14	B	15	C
16	B	17	A	18	A	19	C	20	A
21	C	22	D	23	B	24	D	25	B
26	A	27	B	28	A	29	D	30	C
31	A	32	B	33	A	34	A	35	B
36	C	37	A	38	A	39	B	40	B
41	B	42	D						

If you have won $125,000, well done! Turn to page 213 to play for $250,000!

ANSWERS

$250,000

1	B	2	D	3	D	4	A	5	A
6	D	7	B	8	B	9	B	10	D
11	C	12	B	13	A	14	B	15	A
16	D	17	C	18	B	19	A	20	C
21	C	22	D	23	A	24	A	25	D
26	C	27	A	28	A	29	B	30	A
31	D	32	A	33	B	34	D	35	B
36	C	37	C	38	B				

If you have won $250,000, well done! Turn to page 223 to play for $500,000!

$500,000

1	B	2	A	3	C	4	C	5	D
6	D	7	A	8	C	9	A	10	C
11	D	12	D	13	A	14	C	15	A
16	D	17	A	18	A	19	B	20	C
21	C	22	C	23	C	24	B	25	D
26	D	27	D	28	C	29	B	30	B
31	A	32	D	33	B	34	B		

If you have won $500,000, well done! Turn to page 231 to play for $1,000,000!

$1,000,000

1	D	2	D	3	A	4	A	5	B
6	B	7	D	8	B	9	B	10	C
11	A	12	B	13	C	14	D	15	A
16	B	17	C	18	C	19	C	20	A
21	D	22	A	23	D	24	C	25	A
26	A	27	B	28	C	29	A	30	A

If you have won $1,000,000, well done! You're a millionaire!

Score sheets

Write your name and the names of any other contestants in the space provided. Shade in each of the boxes lightly with a pencil once you or one of your fellow contestants has won the amount in that box. If you or any of the other contestants answer a question incorrectly and are out of the game, use a soft eraser to rub out the relevant boxes so that the final score is showing.

SCORE SHEET

contestant's name		contestant's name	
50:50		50:50	
15	$1 MILLION	15	$1 MILLION
14	$500,000	14	$500,000
13	$250,000	13	$250,000
12	$125,000	12	$125,000
11	$64,000	11	$64,000
10	$32,000	10	$32,000
9	$16,000	9	$16,000
8	$8,000	8	$8,000
7	$4,000	7	$4,000
6	$2,000	6	$2,000
5	$1,000	5	$1,000
4	$500	4	$500
3	$300	3	$300
2	$200	2	$200
1	$100	1	$100

SCORE SHEET

contestant's name

....

50:50

15	$1 MILLION
14	$500,000
13	$250,000
12	$125,000
11	$64,000
10	$32,000
9	$16,000
8	$8,000
7	$4,000
6	$2,000
5	$1,000
4	$500
3	$300
2	$200
1	$100

contestant's name

....

50:50

15	$1 MILLION
14	$500,000
13	$250,000
12	$125,000
11	$64,000
10	$32,000
9	$16,000
8	$8,000
7	$4,000
6	$2,000
5	$1,000
4	$500
3	$300
2	$200
1	$100

SCORE SHEET

contestant's name		contestant's name	
....		....	
50:50		50:50	
15	$1 MILLION	15	$1 MILLION
14	$500,000	14	$500,000
13	$250,000	13	$250,000
12	$125,000	12	$125,000
11	$64,000	11	$64,000
10	$32,000	10	$32,000
9	$16,000	9	$16,000
8	$8,000	8	$8,000
7	$4,000	7	$4,000
6	$2,000	6	$2,000
5	$1,000	5	$1,000
4	$500	4	$500
3	$300	3	$300
2	$200	2	$200
1	$100	1	$100

SCORE SHEET

contestant's name

....

50:50

15	$1 MILLION
14	$500,000
13	$250,000
12	$125,000
11	$64,000
10	$32,000
9	$16,000
8	$8,000
7	$4,000
6	$2,000
5	$1,000
4	$500
3	$300
2	$200
1	$100

contestant's name

....

50:50

15	$1 MILLION
14	$500,000
13	$250,000
12	$125,000
11	$64,000
10	$32,000
9	$16,000
8	$8,000
7	$4,000
6	$2,000
5	$1,000
4	$500
3	$300
2	$200
1	$100

S C O R E S H E E T

contestant's name		contestant's name	
50:50		50:50	
15	$1 MILLION	15	$1 MILLION
14	$500,000	14	$500,000
13	$250,000	13	$250,000
12	$125,000	12	$125,000
11	$64,000	11	$64,000
10	$32,000	10	$32,000
9	$16,000	9	$16,000
8	$8,000	8	$8,000
7	$4,000	7	$4,000
6	$2,000	6	$2,000
5	$1,000	5	$1,000
4	$500	4	$500
3	$300	3	$300
2	$200	2	$200
1	$100	1	$100

SCORE SHEET

contestant's name

....

50:50

15	$1 MILLION
14	$500,000
13	$250,000
12	$125,000
11	$64,000
10	$32,000
9	$16,000
8	$8,000
7	$4,000
6	$2,000
5	$1,000
4	$500
3	$300
2	$200
1	$100

contestant's name

....

50:50

15	$1 MILLION
14	$500,000
13	$250,000
12	$125,000
11	$64,000
10	$32,000
9	$16,000
8	$8,000
7	$4,000
6	$2,000
5	$1,000
4	$500
3	$300
2	$200
1	$100

SCORE SHEET

contestant's name		contestant's name	
....		....	
50:50 ☐ ☐ ☐		50:50 ☐ ☐ ☐	
15	$1 MILLION	15	$1 MILLION
14	$500,000	14	$500,000
13	$250,000	13	$250,000
12	$125,000	12	$125,000
11	$64,000	11	$64,000
10	$32,000	10	$32,000
9	$16,000	9	$16,000
8	$8,000	8	$8,000
7	$4,000	7	$4,000
6	$2,000	6	$2,000
5	$1,000	5	$1,000
4	$500	4	$500
3	$300	3	$300
2	$200	2	$200
1	$100	1	$100

SCORE SHEET

contestant's name ....

50:50

15	$1 MILLION
14	$500,000
13	$250,000
12	$125,000
11	$64,000
10	$32,000
9	$16,000
8	$8,000
7	$4,000
6	$2,000
5	$1,000
4	$500
3	$300
2	$200
1	$100

contestant's name ....

50:50

15	$1 MILLION
14	$500,000
13	$250,000
12	$125,000
11	$64,000
10	$32,000
9	$16,000
8	$8,000
7	$4,000
6	$2,000
5	$1,000
4	$500
3	$300
2	$200
1	$100

SCORE SHEET

contestant's name		contestant's name	
50:50		50:50	
15	$1 MILLION	15	$1 MILLION
14	$500,000	14	$500,000
13	$250,000	13	$250,000
12	$125,000	12	$125,000
11	$64,000	11	$64,000
10	$32,000	10	$32,000
9	$16,000	9	$16,000
8	$8,000	8	$8,000
7	$4,000	7	$4,000
6	$2,000	6	$2,000
5	$1,000	5	$1,000
4	$500	4	$500
3	$300	3	$300
2	$200	2	$200
1	$100	1	$100

SCORE SHEET

contestant's name		contestant's name	
50:50		50:50	
15	$1 MILLION	15	$1 MILLION
14	$500,000	14	$500,000
13	$250,000	13	$250,000
12	$125,000	12	$125,000
11	$64,000	11	$64,000
10	$32,000	10	$32,000
9	$16,000	9	$16,000
8	$8,000	8	$8,000
7	$4,000	7	$4,000
6	$2,000	6	$2,000
5	$1,000	5	$1,000
4	$500	4	$500
3	$300	3	$300
2	$200	2	$200
1	$100	1	$100